The Wayland Library of Science and Technology

COMMUNICATIONS

RHYS LEWIS

Wayland

The Wayland Library of Science and Technology

The Nature of Matter
The Universal Forces
Stars and Galaxies
The Solar System
The Changing Landscape
Air and Oceans
Origins of Life
The Science of Life
Plants and Animals
Animal Behaviour
The Human Machine
Health and Medicine
The Environment
Feeding the World
Raw Materials
Manufacturing Industry
Energy Sources
The Power Generators
Transport
Space Travel
Communications
The Computer Age
Scientific Instruments
Towards Tomorrow

Advisory Series Editor
Robin Kerrod

Consultant
Dr. J. Beynon

Editor: Caroline Sheldrick
Design: David West · Children's Book Design
Picture Research: Alison Renney
Production: Steve Elliott
Art Director: John Ridgeway
Project Director: Lawrence Clarke

First published in 1991 by
Wayland (Publishers) Ltd
61 Western Road, Hove
East Sussex BN3 1JD, England

Planned and produced by:
Andromeda Oxford Limited
The Chambers
11, 13 & 15 Vineyard
Abingdon
Oxon OX14 3PX

British Library Cataloguing in Publication Data
Lewis, Dr Rhys
Communications. – (Wayland library of science and technology)
I. Title II. Series
621.382

ISBN 0-7502-0138-X

Media conversion and typesetting by Peter MacDonald, Una Macnamara and Vanessa Hersey
Origination by Hong Kong Reprohouse Co Ltd
Printed in Italy by Rotolito Lombarda S.p.A., Milan
Bound in France by AGM

Front cover: Compact discs.
Back cover: A video camera.

Contents

LIBRARY
TALLAHASSEE COMMUNITY SCHOOL

Introduction

Communication is as old as the human race. Even before there were recognizable languages, people made sounds and signs to talk to one another. The invention of efficient printing methods in the 1400s allowed people to publish their views and distribute them widely. Since the 1800s there have been great advances in communication technology. First the telegraph and then the telephone put people in touch with one another across cities and continents. Radio became the first means of mass sound communication. Millions of people could be reached in their own homes by broadcasts transmitted from a central studio. In the second half of the century, television has overtaken radio as the main broadcasting medium. Today our planet is circled by satellites high above the Equator. They instantly relay telephone calls, television pictures and other electronic communications.

◀ Compact discs store sound in digital form. They are very accurate and long-lasting. The plastic material is coated with aluminium and then with lacquer for extra protection.

LIBRARY
TALLAHASSEE COMMUNITY SCHOOL

The printed word

Spot facts

- *The Lawrence Livermore Laboratory in California, USA, houses the fastest printer in the world. It can print up to 3.6 million characters per minute: more than 3,000 times as many as the fastest typewriter. It could print The Bible in 65 seconds.*
- *The oldest printed book, a South Korean sutra, or scroll printed with wooden blocks, dates from about AD 700. This was more than 700 years earlier than Gutenberg's Bible, the first book to be mechanically printed, in 1454.*
- *The most modern digital phototypesetters can set up to 30 million characters per hour. By hand, 1,500 characters per hour can be set.*

Every day we are all surrounded by print in newspapers, magazines, books, maps, posters, and countless other things. Printing allows words and pictures to be set down and copied at great speed. It has increased enormously the amount of information that we can now share about our world.

Many thousands of copies of this book have been printed. The words and pictures in the book have to be prepared for printing in a different way and then brought together for the print run to produce the finished book. Colour pictures are printed four times, each time in a different-coloured ink. Similar processes are used for all printed work. Many newspapers are now produced by the most advanced printing methods, using computers and lasers, and include colour pictures.

▶ Each copy of this book contains identical reproductions of the original pictures chosen to illustrate the subjects. As you read this book, other people all round the world can read the same book printed in their own language.

Typesetting

To print a page of a book, a copy of the words first has to be made out of metal. The completed metal letter will be covered in ink and pieces of paper pressed against it to transfer the ink to the page. The traditional way to produce the printed page is for a typesetter to select individual metal letters, each made as a mirror image of the letter to be printed. The case in which all the metal letters are stored has the capital letters in the upper part and the small letters in the lower part. This is why they are sometimes called upper-case and lower-case letters. The metal pieces are picked from the case and the typesetter arranges them in order, upside-down in a hand-held composing stick.

When the row of letters is complete, it is positioned as the bottom line on a frame called a galley. When the next line is complete, it is set above the previous line. The whole page is built up in this way. The finished galley contains an upside-down copy of the original page as it would appear in a mirror. When this is inked and used to print from, the printed page has the lines in the right order and all the letters the right way round.

Modern methods of typesetting avoid the lengthy process of arranging each metal letter individually. The author's writing can be typed into a word- processor and stored on a computer disc. The completed disc is then given to the compositor whose job is to translate the required page layout into computer commands on the disc. This will include details of the line length, spacing between lines, the typeface to be used, and the arrangement of the text on the page. Spaces will be left for pictures to be inserted later.

All these features of the finished page can be finalized on the computer screen without anything having to be printed. When the page of text is complete, the disc is transferred to a machine called a phototypesetter which produces a copy of the finalized text in the correct positions on transparent film. The shapes of all the letters are stored in the memory of the phototypesetter computer. A cathode-ray tube or a laser is used to transfer the shape of the letters required on to the film. This film is used in the manufacture of the metal printing plate, from which the paper page is printed.

► Traditional typesetting, which involves assembling lines of metal characters by hand. Many different styles of type are stored in the bench racks and drawers.

▼ Modern typesetting, which allows editors to change the text and decide on page layout on a computer screen. Phototypesetting machines can then set the type on to film at 1,000 lines per minute.

Origination

Origination is the copying of text or illustrations on to film, from which a printing plate can be made. Modern methods of phototypesetting can produce the film of the finished text directly. Otherwise the text is typeset in the traditional way and, once corrected, a photograph is then taken of a printed page.

Black-and-white photographs are reproduced every day in newspapcrs. They appear to be accurate copies of the original but in fact the printing process used for newspapers cannot print in grey, only in black. All the grey areas in the picture are made up of black dots on a white background (for light grey) or white dots on a black background (for dark grey). The original picture is converted to dots by photographing it through a screen containing many thousands of small holes. This screened photograph is used to make the printing plate.

Full-colour pictures, such as the illustrations in this book, are reproduced in a similar way. Colour pictures are printed using only black and three colours: yellow, cyan (a light blue), and magenta (a light purple), but the printed pictures you can see appear to contain all shades of colour. This is achieved by photographing the original three times through red, green and blue coloured filters. A screened copy of each photograph is then produced as for black-and-white photographs.

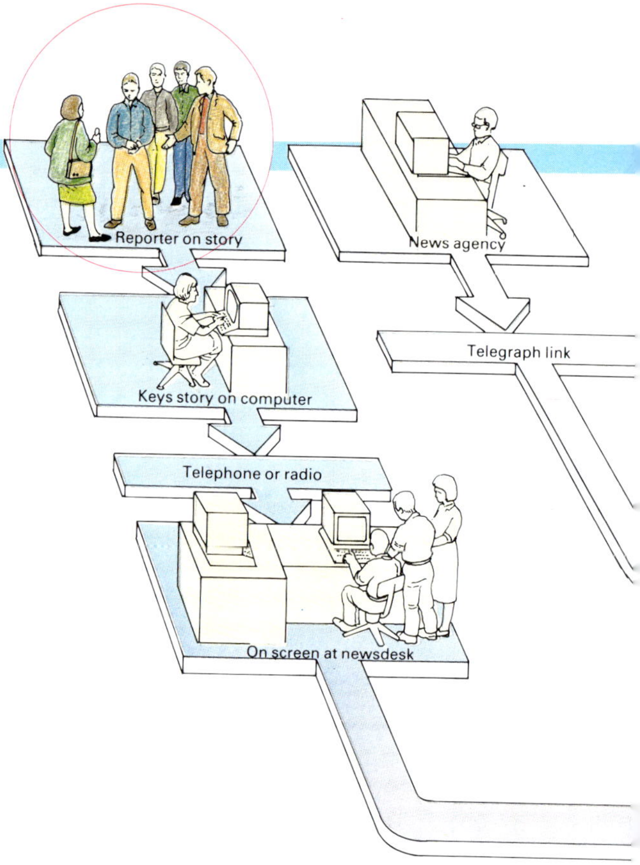

▲ Many newspapers use advanced technology to speed communications. By keeping words, illustrations and photographs stored in a computer, they can be used as required by journalists, editors, designers and printers. Journalists can type their stories directly into the computer. Photographs can also be scanned and entered into the computer. Editors design the layouts of the pages on screen. The finished design can then be typeset and made into film, from which printing plates are made.

► All printed full-colour pictures are made up of three coloured images, one in each of the three colours yellow, magenta and cyan. There is also a black image. These images, when put together, make a full-colour picture. First the full-colour original is photographed in black and white through a green filter. The resulting picture is re-photographed and screened into dots. From this a printing plate is made to be used with magenta-coloured ink. Similarly, using a red filter results in the printing plate for cyan ink, and a blue filter for yellow ink. To print a full-colour picture the paper must undergo four printing processes, one for each coloured ink and one for black ink. The resulting image will be a full-colour picture.

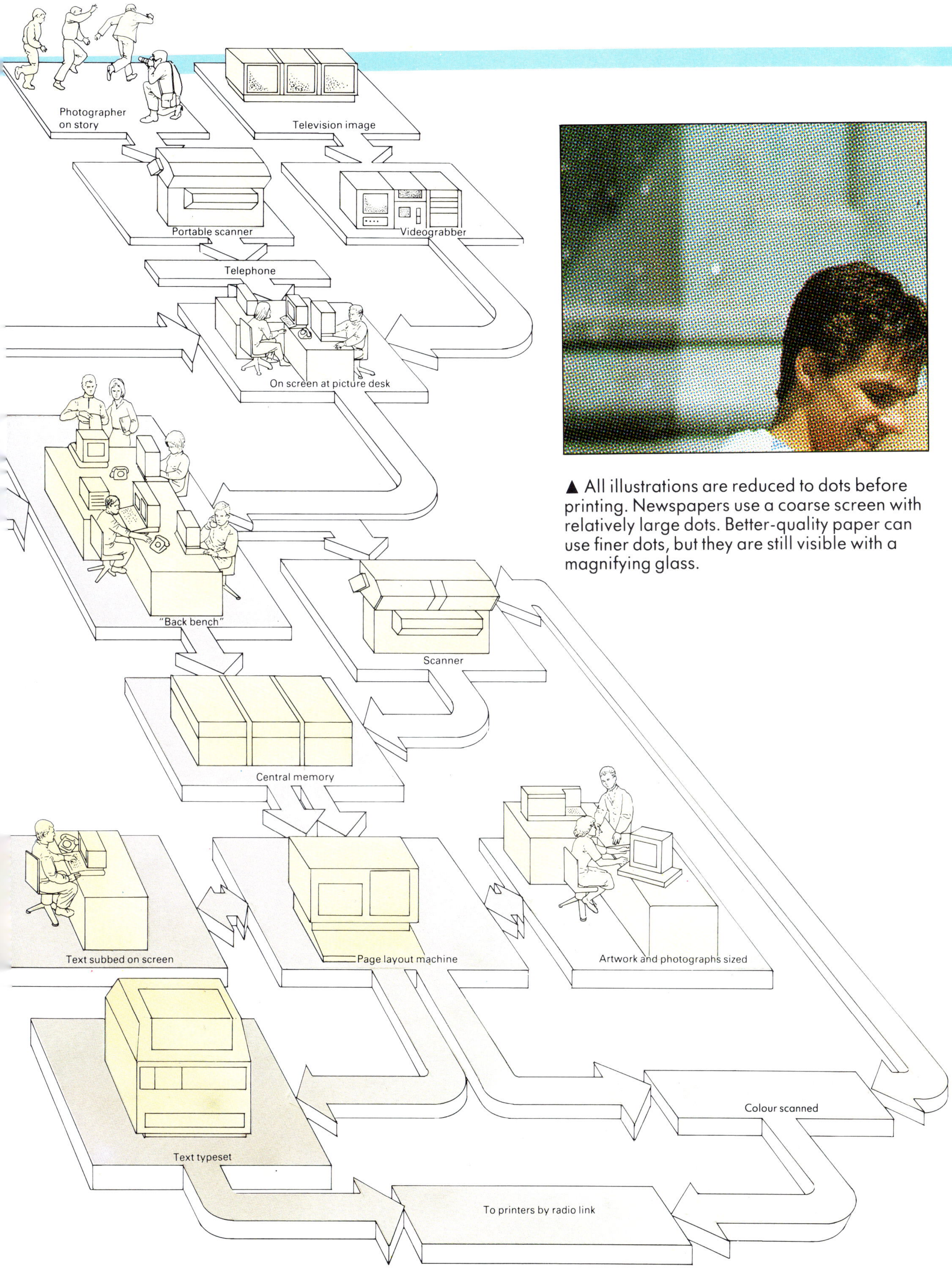

▲ All illustrations are reduced to dots before printing. Newspapers use a coarse screen with relatively large dots. Better-quality paper can use finer dots, but they are still visible with a magnifying glass.

Printing methods

When the text has been typeset and pictures have been screened and made into final film, it is time to make the printing plate from which multiple copies will be made. All printing processes have to be designed to put ink on the paper in the places where it is required and nowhere else. There are three major printing processes, using different techniques to achieve this. These processes are called letterpress, gravure, and offset lithography. Newspapers are printed by offset lithography. Colour supplements are printed by gravure.

Although the printing plates for these processes are different, they are all made in a similar way. A metal plate is covered in a light-sensitive chemical. The transparent film of the page layout is brought close to the plate, and a bright light is shone through the film on to the plate. The chemical reacts where it is exposed to the light and in those areas it binds to the metal, acting as a protective layer on the surface. The metal is then exposed to a chemical process which either removes unprotected metal or changes its surface properties. In both cases the protective layer shields some areas of the metal from attack. The finished printing plates are wrapped around cylinders, which rotate as paper is pulled over them, transferring ink to the paper. A fourth method, silk screen printing, is often used for posters.

Gutenberg

Although books were being printed in China over a thousand years ago, the credit for introducing mass-production printing into Europe must go to Johannes Gutenberg. He lived in Mainz in West Germany in the 1400s. To print a page, the type was placed in a sliding tray and inked. The paper was placed on top, and the press was screwed down. This printing technique remained unchanged for three hundred years until rotating printing presses were invented.

▲ A web offset press prints a continuous roll of paper.

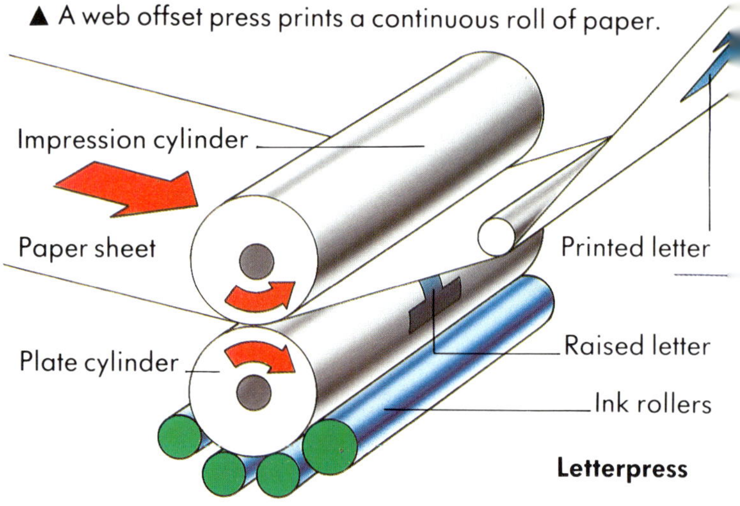

▲ The letterpress method is to etch away from the printing plate those areas which should not be printed. The raised areas are inked and the plate is rolled over the paper.

Ink consists of pigments, which form the colour, and additives, which control properties such as the stickiness or drying speed. A letterpress ink should be tacky and not flow very easily. In the gravure process, the ink must be thin enough to fill all the tiny cavities in the printing plate. It must also be sticky enough so that the ink is pulled out of the cavities when the paper is pressed against the plate. Lithography involves distinguishing between areas of the plate that receive ink and others which are wetted and repel ink. The ink must not run into the water but must fill all the unwetted areas. In all high-speed printing processes, ink needs to dry on the paper quickly.

Photocopying machine

The page to be copied is placed in the machine on a transparent surface. A rotating cylinder is first given a uniform electric charge. A bright light is moved beneath the original and an image of the page is projected on to the cylinder. Charge leaks away from those areas illuminated. A fine black powder is then sprinkled over the cylinder and is attracted to those areas still charged (the black areas). A blank piece of paper is moved over the cylinder, picking up the black powder. Heat then seals the powder on to the page.

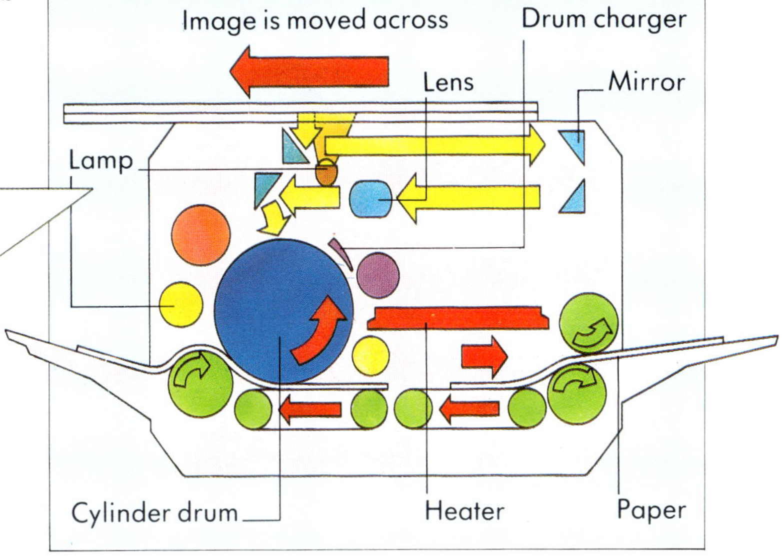

Silk screen

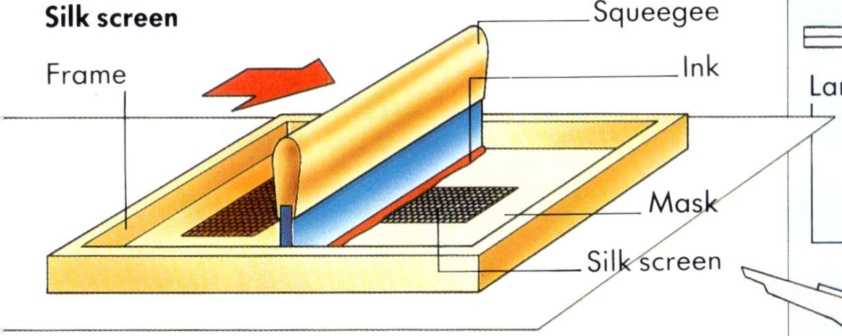

▲ In silk screen printing, ink is squeezed through a stencil onto the material beneath. Around the shape to be printed the stencil is made impervious to ink with a soluble gum.

Gravure

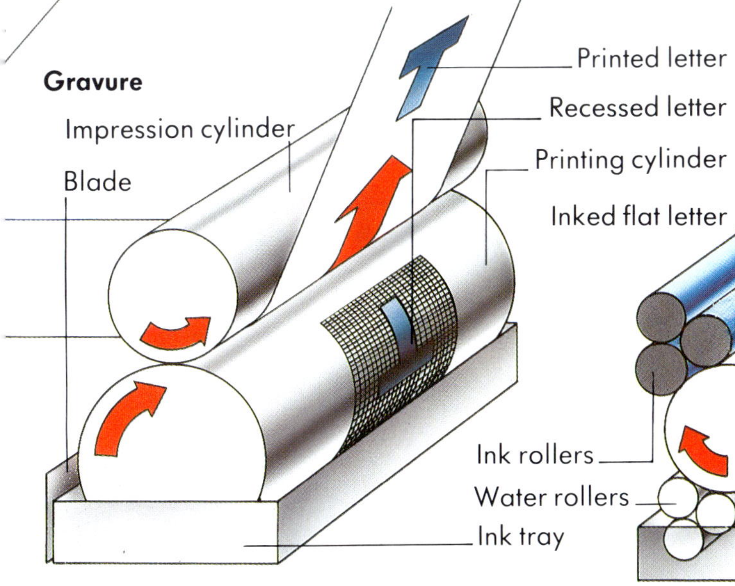

▲ The gravure method is to etch away the area which is to be printed and to fill the etched area with ink. In this technique all text and illustrations have to be screened into dots.

Offset lithography

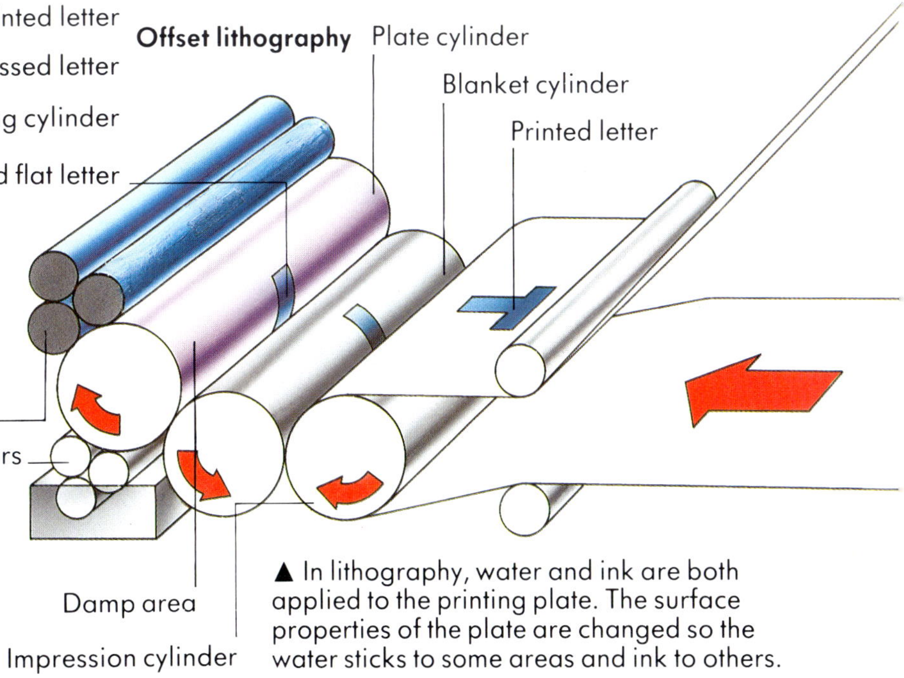

▲ In lithography, water and ink are both applied to the printing plate. The surface properties of the plate are changed so the water sticks to some areas and ink to others.

Photography

Spot facts

- *The finest microfiche is able to display up to 6,000 frames on a single sheet 10 cm by 15 cm. The whole telephone directory for a large city can be stored on one sheet.*

- *The fastest camera in the world is used in laser research at the Blackett Laboratory, London. It is able to take up to 33 billion images per second.*

- *The oldest surviving colour photograph was taken in 1877.*

- *Twinkling stars which appear white to the naked eye can be seen in full colour by means of long-exposure astrophotography.*

- *The original daguerreotypes needed up to 20 minutes' exposure in strong sunlight, but the film in a standard modern pocket camera is 36,000 times as fast, with an exposure time of only 1/30 of a second.*

► Athletes at speed. By careful choice of camera lens and technique, the photographer can capture the spirit as well as the substance of the subject being photographed.

Photography is the science and art of permanently recording pictures of the world. A photograph can remind you of someone you love or bring back memories of things that are past. Photographs can be beautiful, impressive, informative or funny. The complicated chemistry of photography has been mastered so completely that photographs can be taken, developed and printed in less than a minute. Cameras have advanced so far that they can now operate completely automatically. Photography also allows us to look at things which we cannot see with our eyes alone because they move too quickly, too slowly, or are too far away. Photography is a means of mass communication also open to individuals.

Drawing with light

It is very simple to see an image of a brightly-lit scene on a screen. The screen must be in a dark box with a small pinhole in the box, through which the light from the outside world can come to illuminate the screen. If the pinhole is the right size, there will be an image of the scene outside focused on the screen. This was known thousands of years ago. The device was called a camera obscura which means "dark room". Although producing the image is simple, it is much more difficult to invent a screen which will permanently record the picture. This is the process of photography, which literally means "drawing with light".

The first ever photograph was taken in the year 1826 by a French soldier called Joseph Nicéphore Niépce. He recorded the view from his window on a metal plate, which had been coated with a light-sensitive substance. He had to wait all day for the picture to appear on the metal plate because the sensitivity of the coating on the plate was so low. Also, he did not use a lens to concentrate the light on to the metal plate. Soon afterwards he went into partnership with another Frenchman, who was called Louis Daguerre.

After Niépce's death, Daguerre invented a much more sensitive method of recording pictures, using copper plates coated with silver. The plates were first exposed to iodine fumes, which made the surface light-sensitive. The picture was taken and then the plates were exposed to mercury vapour, which brought out the picture on the plate. The picture was fixed permanently by washing the plate in salty water.

Because the new coating was more sensitive to light, pictures could be taken more quickly. The reduced exposure times allowed photographs of people to be taken for the first time. The portraits were called daguerreotypes after their inventor and were very popular.

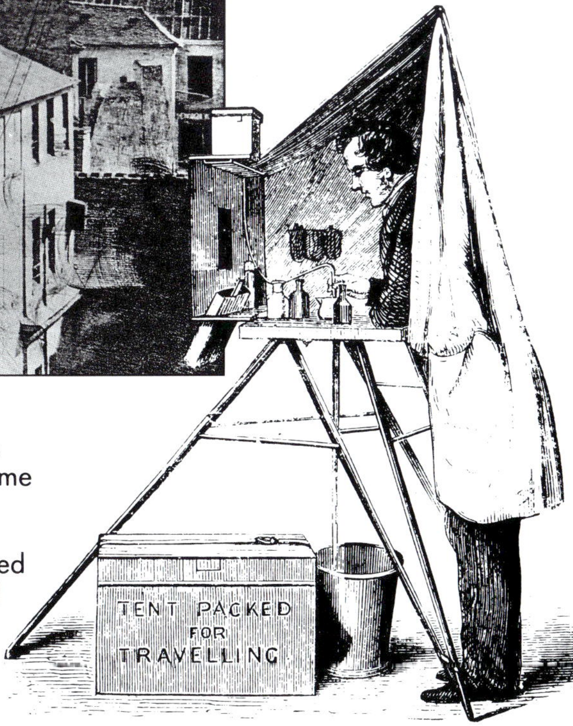

▲ This daguerreotype picture of a street in Paris was taken by Daguerre himself in 1833. It includes the first photographed human figure. Early photographs such as this one required very long exposure times. The man in the picture stood still to have his boots cleaned for long enough for his image to be recorded on the photographic plate.

► A new photographic technique was invented in 1851, which became more popular than the daguerreotype. It was called the wet-collodion process and involved coating a glass plate with a liquid and then exposing it to the light. Photographers had to carry chemicals with them and coat the plate inside the camera.

Negatives and positives

The first photographers were trying to find a way of recording a picture as a "positive" image. They wanted a process which would record the bright areas of the screen as white in the photograph and dark areas as black. (All early photographs were black and white.) This proved to be very difficult.

A breakthrough was made by an Englishman, William Fox Talbot. He found a relatively simple way of first producing a "negative" of the photograph, and then making a positive picture from the negative. His method of printing was very similar to that still used today, and allows many prints to be made from a single negative.

Modern photographic film consists of a thin layer, or emulsion, of a chemical called a silver halide, on a transparent plastic sheet. The chemical is a combination of atoms of silver, and atoms of one of the elements bromine, chlorine, iodine or fluorine. These chemicals are sensitive to light. Normally transparent, they become black if they are exposed to light, or illuminated, so the film naturally records a negative picture in which the brightest areas of the scene produce the darkest area on the film.

A positive print can be made from the negative by placing the negative on a new piece of film and illuminating the film through the negative. This is called a contact print. The darkest areas of the negative produce the lightest areas on the print. If a print is required which is larger than the negative, the negative is held away from the film. Light shining through the negative then produces a larger image of it on the film.

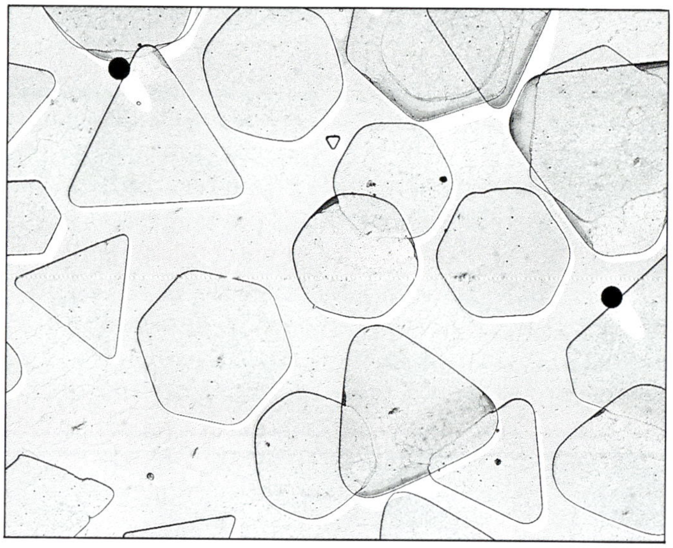

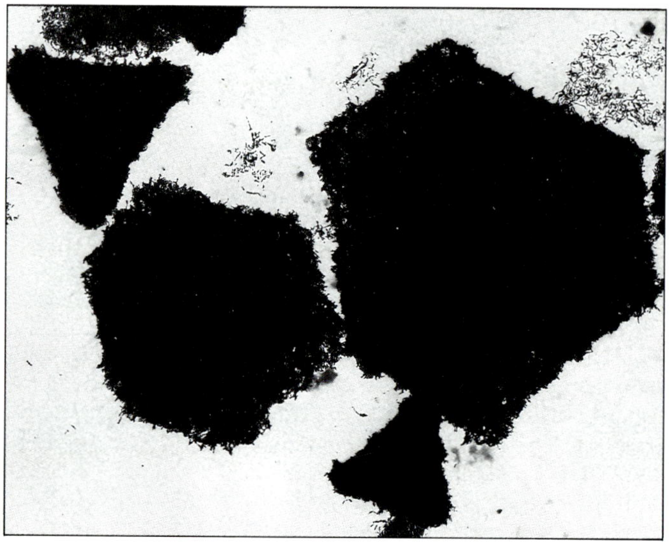

► (top) A highly-magnified view of a piece of unexposed photographic film, showing the crystals of silver halide. When light falls on the film, it produces some atoms of metallic silver within the crystals. (middle) Two crystals in which small areas have been blackened. If the exposed film was examined at this stage, there would be no picture to see. The film now has to be developed by immersing it in a chemical solution. In this solution the crystals blacken completely if they have been at all affected by light. (bottom) Crystals in the film after it has been developed. The picture is now visible on the film. The film is then immersed in a different solution which washes away all the unblackened crystals of silver halide. The film is no longer sensitive to light, and the picture is permanently fixed in the film.

Colour photography

Colour photography also uses crystals of silver halide as the light-sensitive material in which to record a picture. Colour film contains three layers of silver halide crystals. Each layer also contains chemicals which can form coloured dyes. When the film is exposed to light, each layer reacts only to red, green, or blue light. After the film has been developed, each layer contains coloured dye in the same places as the silver halide has been turned to silver. The dye colours are the complementary colours of those in the original image. For example, blue light results in yellow dye, and green light results in a magenta dye. The developed film therefore contains a colour negative of the image.

▼ In colour photography, the multi-layered film is developed using a chemical which produces different coloured dyes in the exposed parts of each layer. To print the image, white light is shone through the negative on to paper having a similar multi-layer coating. This reverses the colours, and the final print shows the same colours as the original image.

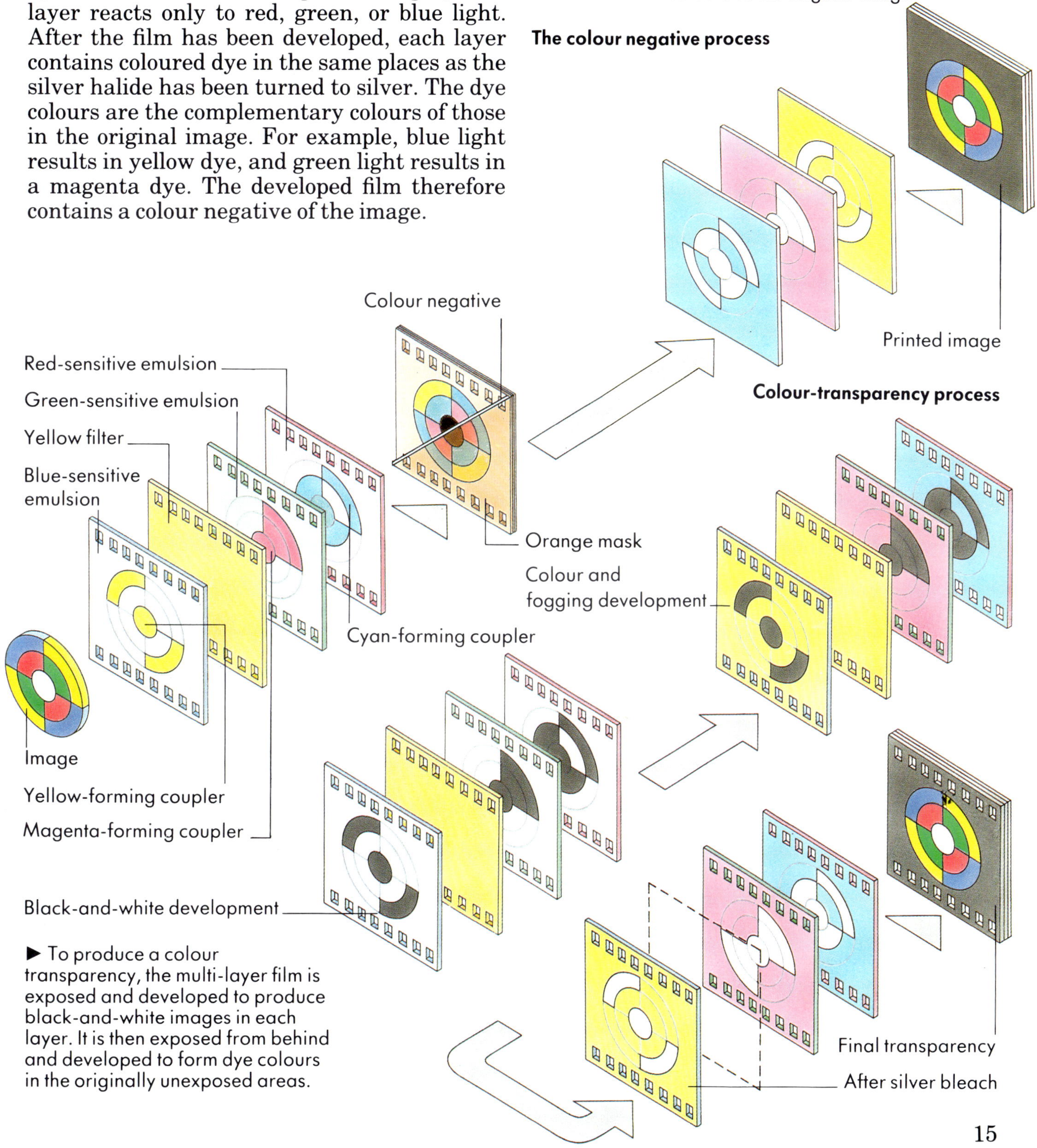

► To produce a colour transparency, the multi-layer film is exposed and developed to produce black-and-white images in each layer. It is then exposed from behind and developed to form dye colours in the originally unexposed areas.

Cameras

The first cameras were simple devices consisting of a box which held a single plate of film, and a lens to focus light on to the film. Modern cameras can be extremely sophisticated electronic machines with many functions automatically controlled. However, the principles of the camera are still the same. A roll of film loads into the back of the camera. Inside the camera it is completely dark until a picture is taken. A shutter inside the camera then opens to allow light coming through the lens to fall on the film. After a short time the shutter closes and the film can then be wound on to move an unexposed piece of film into position behind the shutter and lens. The main controls available to the photographer are the lens position, the lens aperture size and the exposure time.

Light from the scene to be photographed is focused on to the film by the lens, or group of lenses, to produce a sharp image of the subject. However, light coming from objects at different distances will focus at different positions behind the lens. To focus on subjects closer to the camera, the lens body is rotated, which screws it away from the camera body and the film. The aperture size is set by rotating a ring at the back of the lens.

Reducing the aperture will reduce the amount of light reaching the film. To compensate, the exposure time (the time for which the shutter is open) can be varied between a few seconds, for very dark scenes, to one-thousandth of a second. The very fast speed is used to photograph fast-moving objects so they do not appear blurred. Most cameras can automatically set the exposure time after the aperture size has been chosen. The amount of light in the scene is measured inside the camera, and the exposure time is set to allow the same amount of light always to hit the film.

Pocket camera

The modern pocket camera is designed to be easy to use. The photographer composes a picture in the viewfinder and presses the shutter-release button. The shutter opens for a fraction of a second to expose one frame of the film, which captures an image of the scene viewed. Working the film-advance lever moves another frame of the film into position behind the shutter. The time of exposure is calculated automatically. A built-in light meter records the light level, and, acting on this information, the camera alters the shutter speed and/or lens aperture to give the correct exposure. The lens aperture is set by the iris diaphragm. This is made up of overlapping metal leaves, which advance or retract, depending on whether less or more light needs to enter. In low-level lighting conditions flash must be used to give adequate exposure. A flash gun is fixed into the "hot-shoe", which has electrical contacts that cause the flash to be set off when the shutter opens.

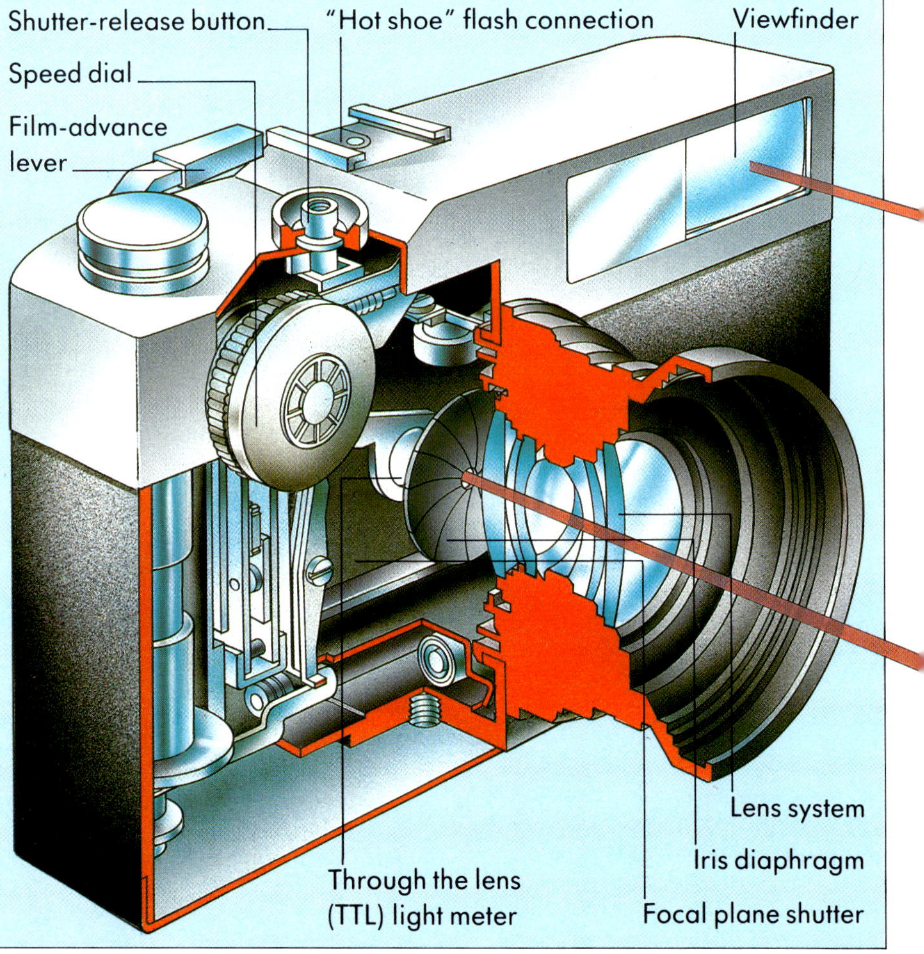

► This is an early camera, built in 1856, which used the collodion process. A plate of glass would be fitted inside the back of the camera to record a single picture. The lens could be moved to focus the image. The chemicals needed to sensitize the glass were then put in the top of the camera. After the plate had been exposed to the image, further chemicals would be squeezed into the camera to process the photograph.

▼ The main type of camera in use today is the single lens reflex (SLR) camera. The SLR camera has only one lens (although this may consist of many optical components). The SLR camera can be fitted with many different types of lens: zoom, telephoto, macro, fisheye, which allow great variation in the focusing distance and in the angle of view of the camera. Many designs have automatic control of aperture size or shutter speed.

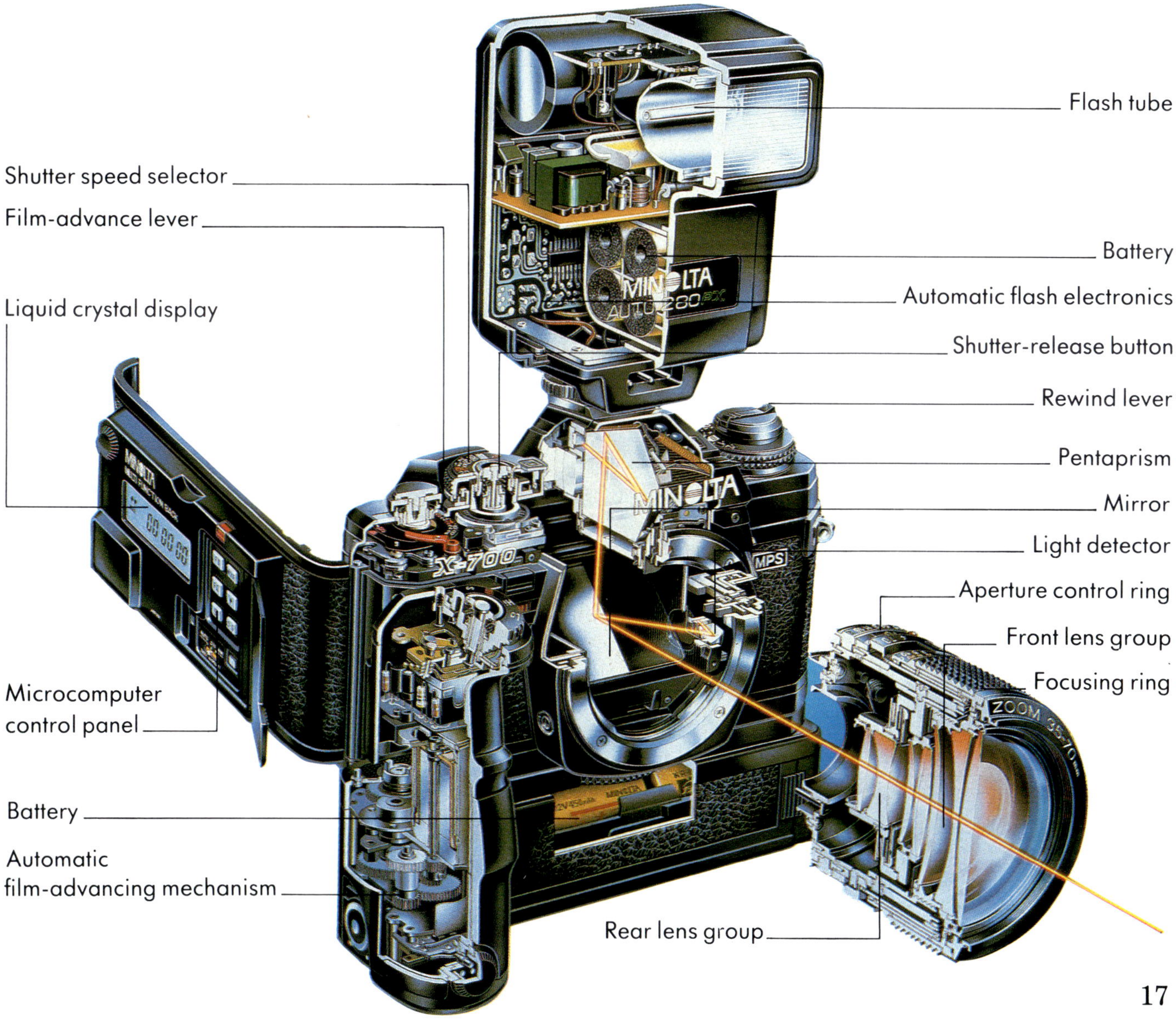

Advanced techniques

Photography was invented as a way of permanently recording scenes that people could see. Modern photography allows us to do much more than this. Pictures can be taken of things that we are unable to see. The normal human eye is sensitive to only a small range of the wavelengths of light. The shortest wavelength we can see is violet light; the longest is red light. Photographic film is not limited to this range. It can be designed to be sensitive to infrared wavelengths (longer than red) and ultraviolet wavelengths (shorter than violet). Some film can record wavelengths even shorter than ultraviolet, of which the most common to be used in photography are called X-rays.

Photography also allows us to overcome other limiting features of the human eye. Some things happen too quickly to be seen, other things happen too slowly. High-speed photography and time-lapse photography make these events visible. High-speed photography involves taking a large number of pictures in a short time. It is important that in each picture, the fast-moving object appears to be stationary so that the image is not blurred. This is achieved by using a flashing light as the illumination for the object. Each flash is a very short burst of bright light, which can repeat thousands of times a second.

Time-lapse photography involves taking frames of a film with long intervals between them. The film sequence is then played back at a much faster rate to speed up the apparent motion. This is a popular technique for showing such things as the growth of plants.

The human eye is also unable to see in very low levels of light. However, using photography, it is possible to build up a picture on sensitive film by collecting light over many hours. All the light hitting the film is recorded and contributes to the finished picture. This method is used in astronomical photography, for example in photographing dim and distant objects in the sky.

▼ A dragonfly in flight captured by high-speed photography. The exposure time is so short that the rapidly moving wings appear motionless.

X-rays

X-rays are used to photograph internal regions of the body. X-rays are a form of electromagnetic radiation with a wavelength roughly one-thousandth that of visible light. The X-rays pass easily through soft tissue but are partly blocked by teeth and bones. Images of the teeth and bones show on X-ray film placed behind a body.

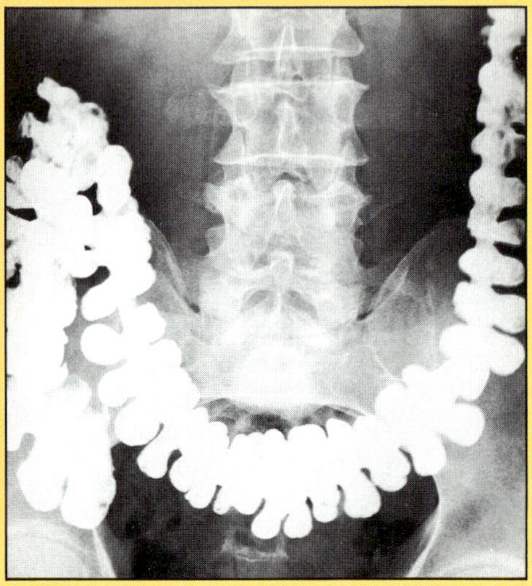

Moving-picture camera

A movie camera takes a large number of pictures on a long reel of film. When the film is played back at sufficient speed through a projector, the human brain does not see that each frame is separate. We receive an impression of smooth motion on the screen. To take the pictures, the film is fed into the camera by the rotation of the spools. The spools rotate continuously, but another mechanism stops the film behind the aperture for long enough for the exposure to be made. The film is then allowed to move on so that the next unexposed frame is brought into position. The camera takes twenty-five frames every second, with each exposure time being one-fiftieth of a second. In the fiftieth of a second following each exposure, the film has to be moved on and stopped again, ready for the next exposure.

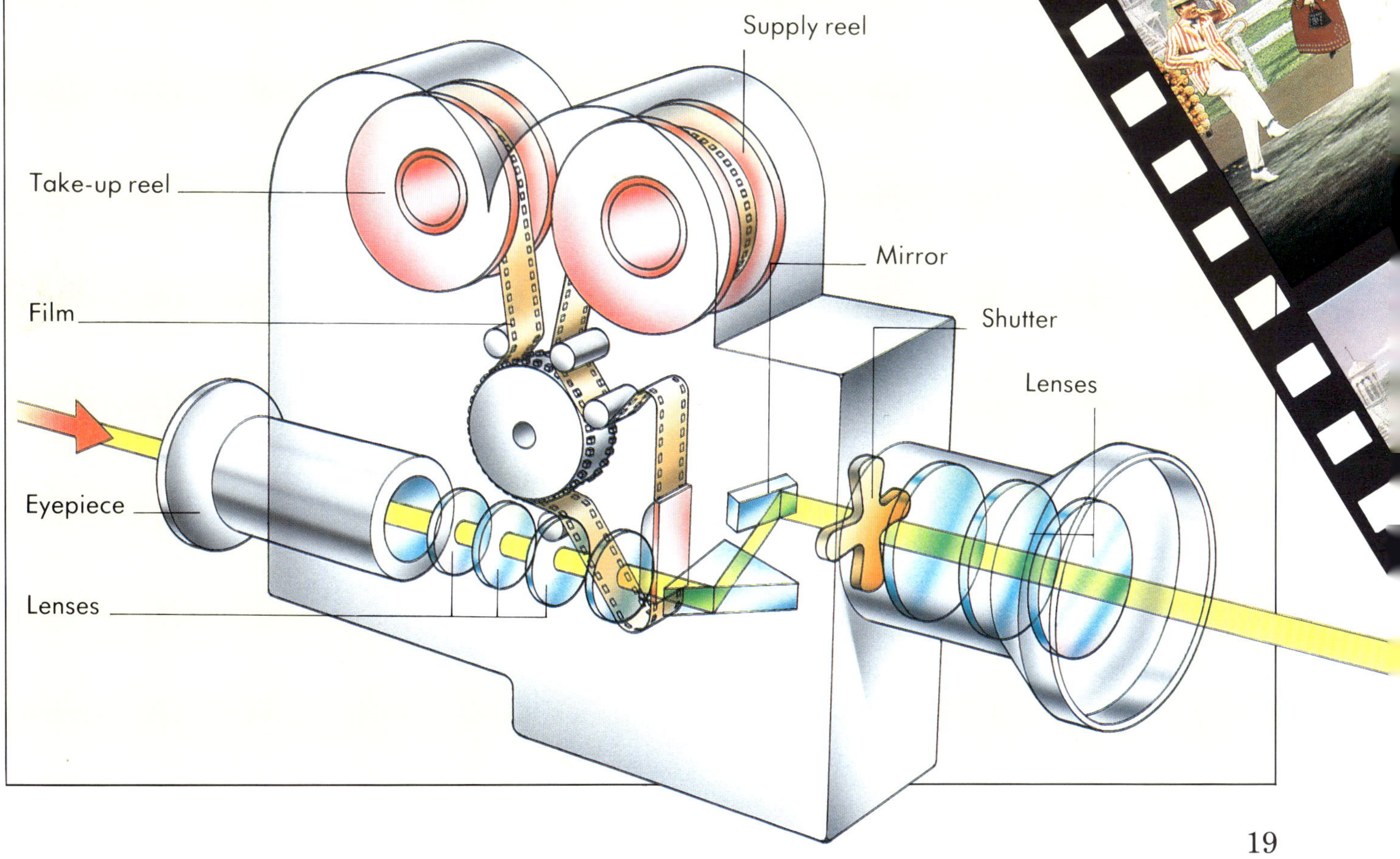

Telecommunications

Spot facts

- *Transmission along the latest optical fibres can accommodate up to 20,000 telephone calls at a time.*
- *The craze for "videotex", or screen-based information systems, has been very successful in France. Over 10 million households have a miniature video terminal, or Minitel.*
- *Early Morse sets were able to transmit about 35 words per minute.*
- *The largest ever private telegraph system was operated by the US armed forces, with 2,700 centres in North and South America and 1,600 other centres around the world.*

From the telephone in any house or office in a major city, a caller can dial a series of numbers and in a few seconds be connected to any telephone in one of a hundred different countries of the world. The telephone network provides a means of communication which is personal. Printing, television, radio and recording are means of mass communication. The telephone system works through a vast network of cables which cross countries, continents and oceans. Microwave stations beam our telephone calls through the air. Satellites are used to relay calls at the speed of light from one country to another. Telephone lines can also be used to carry digital information between computers.

▶ Talking on the telephone is the most personal form of telecommunication. Telephones can bring together in an instant people who may be thousands of kilometres apart at the opposite ends of the Earth.

Signals by wire

Electricity was first used in machines in the first half of the last century. One of the first useful applications of electricity was the construction of a device which could make the voltage at the end of a long wire the same as the voltage at the beginning. Normally the voltage would decrease along the wire because of the electrical resistance of the wire. The new system worked by using the low-voltage strength remaining at the end of the cable to trigger an amplifying device. This boosted the signal back to its original strength to start the journey towards the next amplifying station. A scheme like this is necessary for all long-distance communications whether they are by wire and optical fibre.

The first electrical communications machine used two magnetic needles (like the needle of a compass) which were deflected in different directions, depending on the voltage signals it received along the wires from the sending machine. The same machine could both send and receive signals. The operator had to learn that each letter of the message was represented by a certain number of needle deflections.

The next advance was made by Alfred Vail and Samuel Morse, who installed the first of their communications systems in 1844. This used a code for each letter of the alphabet, consisting of a certain combination of dots and dashes. Common letters such as E and T were given short codes. Uncommon letters were given the long codes. (For example T is "–", while Q is "–.–".) The operator sending the message would translate it into this Morse code during transmission and would tap out the code directly on an electrical contact of the sending device. The receiving device made a click for each tap of the contact. Two clicks close together indicated a dot, two further apart indicated a dash. Very high speeds could be achieved by skilled operators.

Many businesses have telex machines to provide a written record of telecommunications. A telex machine consists of a keyboard, a display screen and a printer. The operator types the message and can check it on the screen. The message is transmitted as a series of on-off voltage pulses. The receiving machine decodes these pulses and prints out the message.

▼ An early design of Morse code receiver. The electrical signals arriving at the receiver would make a pen write dots or dashes on to paper. Later designs simply made clicks for dots and dashes and the receiving operator wrote the message out.

▲ A two-needle telegraph, invented in England in 1837. This was the first practically instantaneous communications method between people who could not see each other. Experienced operators could read up to 20 words a minute.

The telephone

When you speak, you make sound waves in the air. The sound waves can be detected by the human ear so other people can hear what you are saying. The telephone is an instrument which can also respond to the sound waves of your voice and convert them into electrical signals. The signals travel along wires to the receiving telephone, where they are converted back into sound waves. These sound waves have to be similar to the original ones so that the person listening can understand what is being said.

The handset of a telephone consists of a microphone at one end and a loudspeaker at the other. When you speak into the microphone, the impact of the sound waves makes the surface vibrate. Behind the surface of the mouthpiece is a small chamber full of pieces of carbon. As the surface vibrates, the volume of the chamber changes and the carbon granules become more or less tightly packed. This changes the electrical resistance of the carbon. A current flows through one of the wires that comes into the telephone. As the carbon resistance changes, the electric current in this wire also changes. It is this electric current which carries the record of the voice of the person using the phone. The changing electric current travels down wires and is routed by the telephone exchange to the right telephone.

When the current arrives at the receiving phone, it passes through coils wrapped round a magnet in the earpiece. The changing current produces in turn a changing magnetic field in the receiver. This either pulls or pushes a diaphragm, positioned behind the earpiece of the receiver. The vibrating surface reproduces the sound waves which were originally responsible for the varying current. Although the reproduction is not perfect, somebody listening can usually understand what was said into the calling telephone.

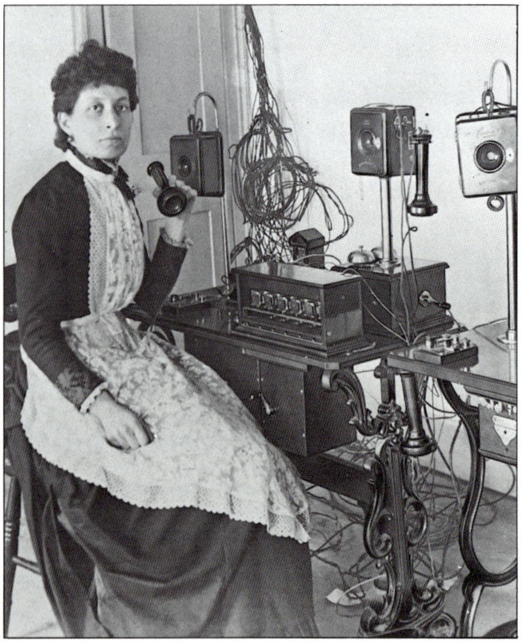

▲ Early telephone exchanges were run by operators connecting calls by hand. This was a slow process, and prone to mistakes.

► Modern telephone exchanges are all electronic. Connections to the dialled telephone number are made automatically. Human intervention is only needed for maintenance.

Telephone network

► At the receiving end of the telephone, a changing magnetic field vibrates a diaphragm in response to the electric signals it receives. The diaphragm sets up sound waves in the air which closely resemble those spoken by the caller.

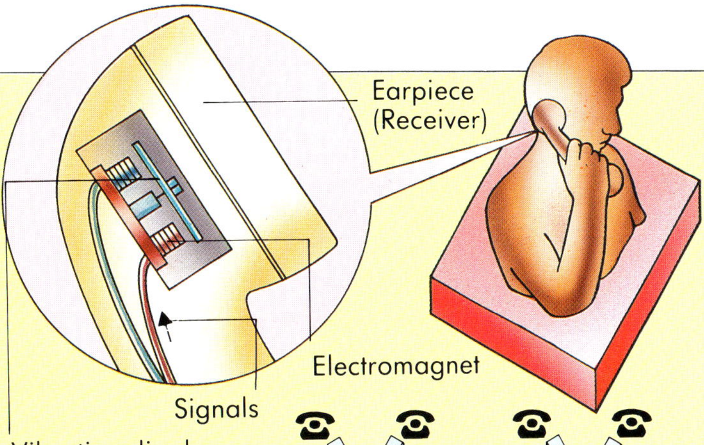

► Every telephone in the world has a number. Each telephone is connected by wires to a local exchange. In a large city the local exchanges are all connected to a central exchange for the city. Each city or area can be called from every other area.

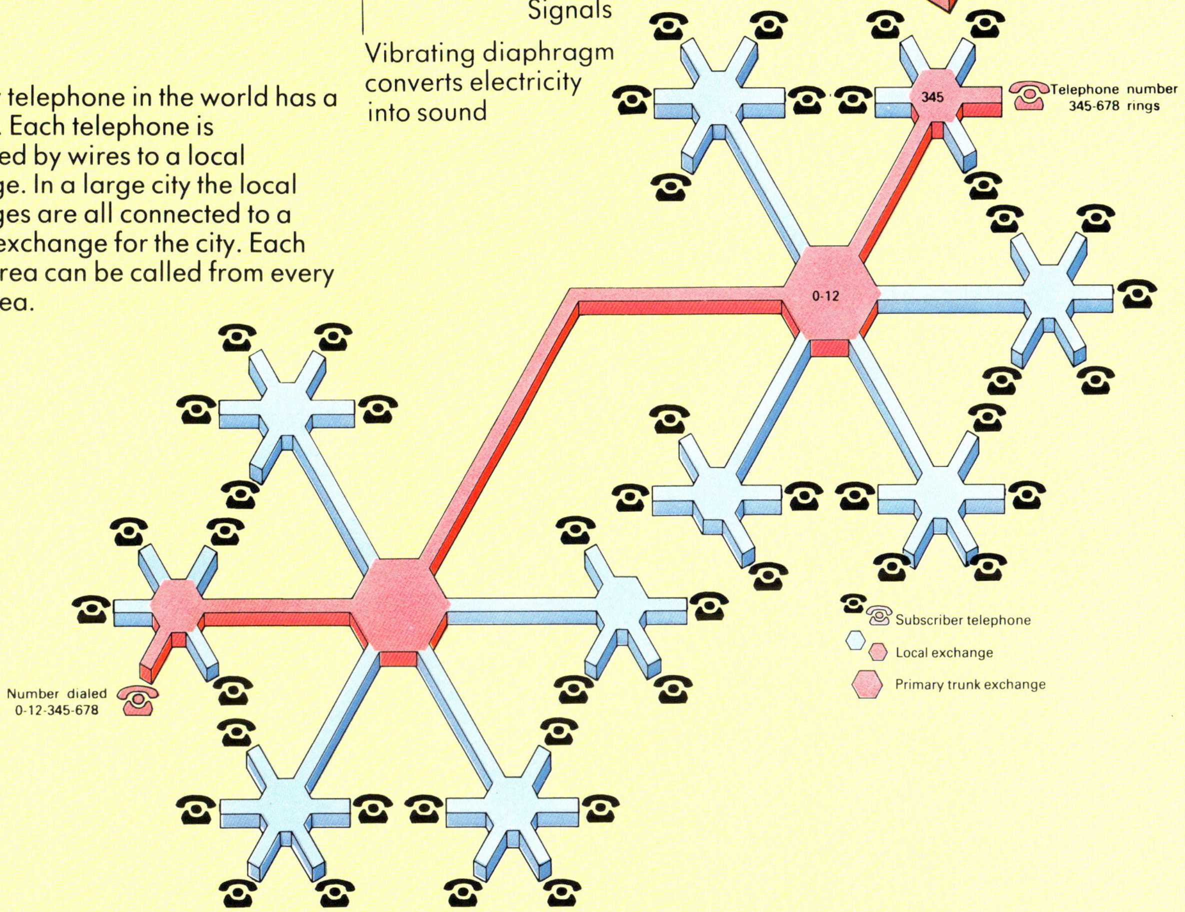

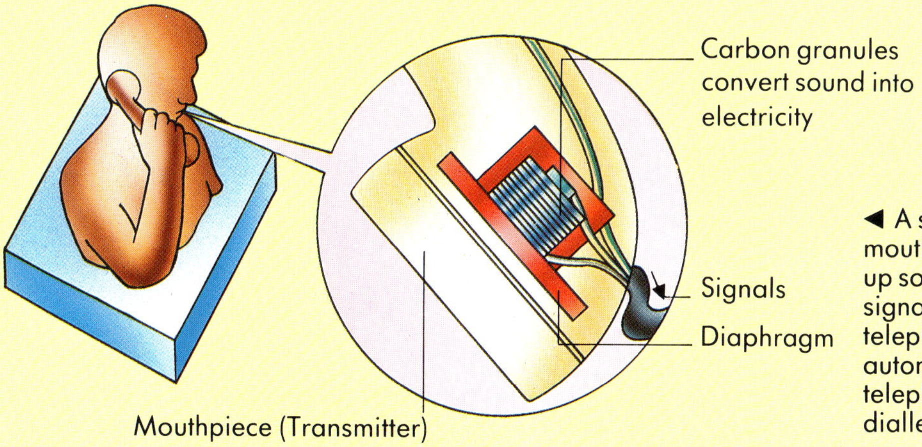

◄ A small microphone in the mouthpiece of the telephone picks up sound and turns it into electrical signals. The signals are fed into the telephone exchange and automatically routed to the telephone whose number was dialled by the caller.

Cable links

Individual telephones are connected by a two-wire cable to a distribution point, usually on a pole in the street. These distribution points are in turn connected to a local cabinet. This combines all local lines into main cables running under the road to the exchange. Local exchanges throughout the country are connected by coaxial cable. This consists of a central conductor surrounded by an electrically insulating plastic which is itself surrounded by a conducting cylinder.

Multiplexing

Because of the expense of laying cables and the increasing demand for telephone lines, it has been important to develop ways of using a single cable for many telephone calls at a time. This is called multiplexing. A common system of multiplexing involves pulse code modulation (PCM). Instead of sending the complete telephone signal along the cable, the strength of the signal is measured eight thousand times a second. This is called digitizing the signal. Each value of signal strength is represented as an eight-digit binary number consisting of ones and zeros. These numbers are sent along the cable and the original signal is reconstructed at the receiver. Because the binary number can be transmitted very rapidly, the cable is only being used for a very short period every one eight-thousandth of a second to transmit information for one telephone call. It is possible to send many other calls at the same time along the same cable by interleaving signal strength

▼ A chaotic mass of telephone cables in 1909 Kansas, United States. When telephones were first invented, every telephone had to be connected to every other telephone by two wires. Even after the installation of local exchanges, every simultaneous call into the exchange had to arrive by a different wire. The solution to this problem arrived with the invention of multiplexing.

information from other telephones.

There are cables which carry telephone calls across seas and oceans. The cables lie on the seabed and have to be strong enough to withstand the huge pressure of water pressing down upon them. The first cable across the Atlantic Ocean was laid in 1956 and could carry up to 36 simultaneous telephone calls. There are now 14 cables which cross between Europe and the American continent. The latest transatlantic telephone cable is called TAT-8. It is an optical-fibre link and can carry up to 40,000 calls at the same time.

► A telecommunications cable made up of optical fibres: thin, flexible glass threads. Optical-fibre cables are now laid by telecommunications companies in preference to copper ones. They have many times the capacity of copper cables, being able to carry up to 20,000 telephone calls at once. The glass used for making optical fibres is so pure that a block 20 km thick would be transparent.

Optical-fibre transmission

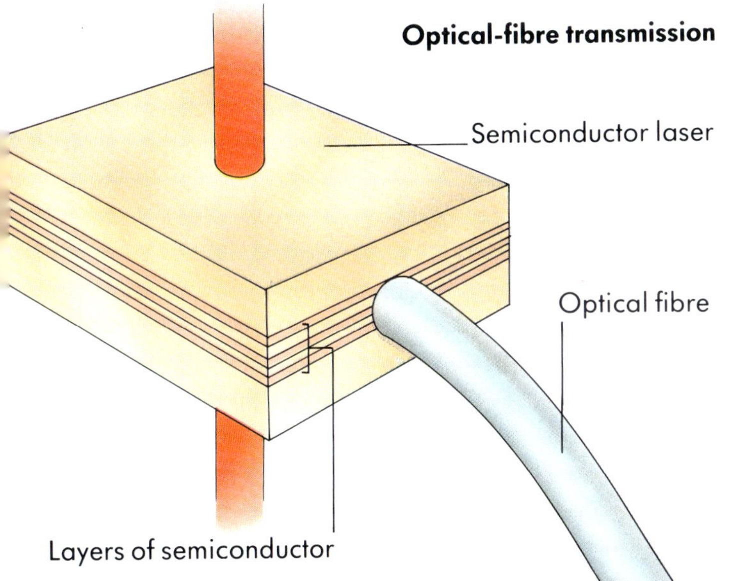
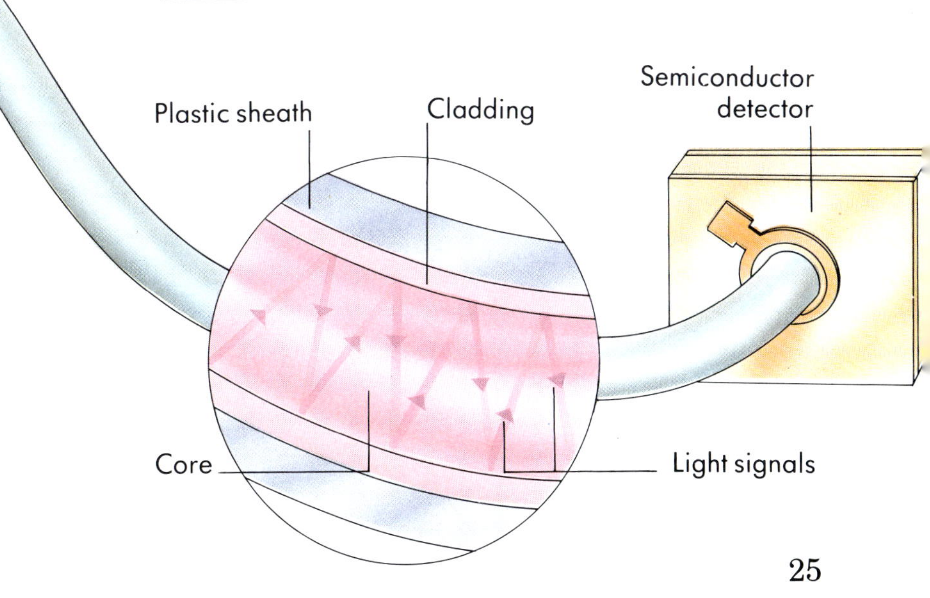

▲ Optical fibres are made from pure quartz glass. This material can be drawn out into very long strands with a small diameter. The fibre is surrounded by a cladding and also a plastic sheath. Pulses of light are sent into the fibre by laser, and travel through it by bouncing off the inside wall of the fibre. The design of the fibre ensures that no light escapes through the side wall. The latest transatlantic telephone cable (photo) uses optical fibres and has a much greater capacity than earlier copper cables.

Microwave links

Microwaves are a form of radiation which have a wavelength longer than visible light but shorter than radio waves. The wavelengths used in communications are between 5 cm and 10 cm. The minimum range for a channel is about 3 kHz (3,000 Hz, or cycles per second). Any region of the frequency spectrum which is 3 kHz wide can be used to transmit a telephone call. A carrier frequency can be added to the spoken frequencies before transmission, and then subtracted after reception to return the range to audible sound. All communications systems have a range of frequencies which they can transmit. This range is called the bandwidth. Splitting the bandwidth into different channels to carry different information is called frequency division multiplexing. Microwaves have a frequency of 3-6 million kHz (3-6 GHz) and so thousands of phone calls can occupy a bandwidth only a small fraction of this.

Microwaves are used to transmit telephone calls through the air. They can be focused to a beam and sent between transmitters and receivers over 50 km apart. They are also used in satellite communications. The signals are sent up to the satellite with a bandwidth centred around a frequency of 4 GHz. The signals are amplified and returned around a central frequency of 6 GHz.

Most communications satellites are geostationary. They orbit the Earth at a height of nearly 36,000 km above the same point.

▲ A microwave relay tower in Florida, USA. Beams of microwaves carrying telephone calls are captured in the detectors, called horns, which are mounted on top of the tower. The signals can then be amplified and redirected to other receiving towers or passed into the cable telephone system.

Long-distance radio transmission

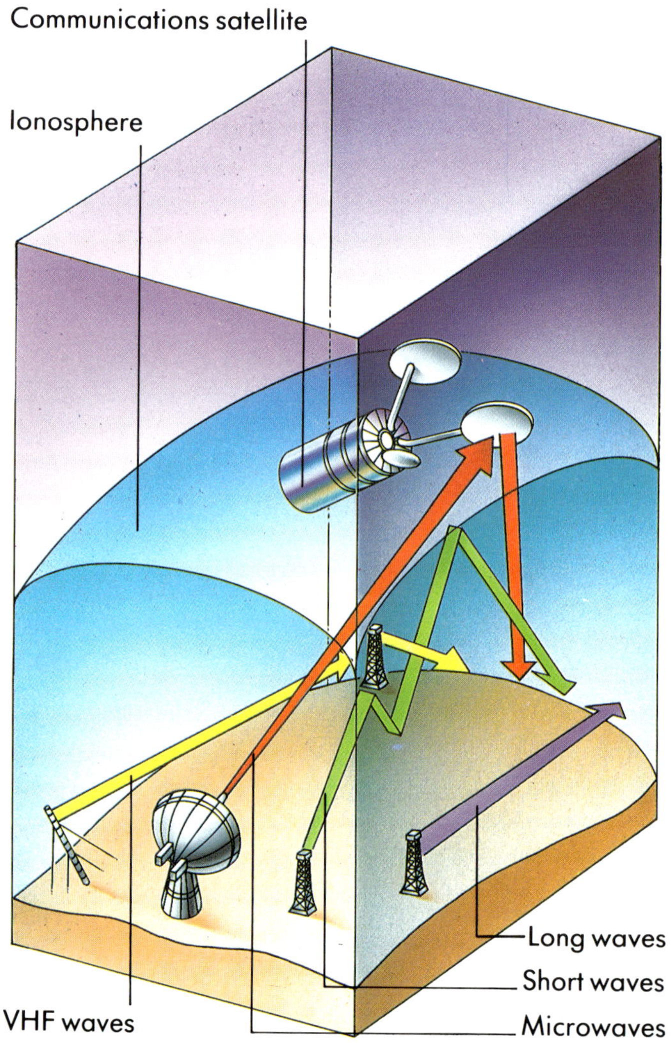

► Very high frequency (VHF) waves are sent in straight lines between tall towers, or bounced off orbiting satellites. Short waves can be made to bounce back to Earth from the ionosphere.

Fax and electronic mail

Both facsimile (known as fax) and electronic mail (e-mail) are ways of sending documents without using the conventional postage system. Both are much faster than ordinary mail, and both make use of telephone lines to transmit information. Fax and e-mail use a device called a modem (short for modulator-demodulator). The modem converts digital information from a fax machine or a computer into a sound signal which can be sent down a telephone line. A modem at the other end of the line changes this signal back to the original format.

The fax machine can transmit any document, whether it contains words or pictures. The document is placed face down on the machine which then pulls it over a strip of bright light. A scanner measures the reflectivity of the paper. White areas reflect the light much more than areas with writing or drawing on them. This information is recorded in a sequence of numbers. For each small area of paper, a one or a zero is added to the sequence depending on whether the page is light or dark at that point. This information is then sent along a telephone line to the receiving fax machine, where it is used to copy the original page.

E-mail provides a way for people with computers to communicate with each other. A computer can be linked to the telephone system using a modem. The sender types out the message and instructs the computer to send it. The information is converted into a signal for transmission down a telephone line. At the destination computer, the signal may be reconverted and shown on the receiver's screen at once. Or if that computer is turned off or in use, the message can be stored in the central memory bank for later retrieval. By this method messages can be transmitted purely as electronic signals, without ever being printed.

Facsimile system

The scanner reads the information of light and dark on the document. The information is coded into binary digits, then converted by a modem into a telephone signal. Transmitted via a relay tower, the signal is reconverted to a binary sequence at the receiving end. The receiving fax machine then creates a duplicate of the original document by exposing light-sensitive paper to bright illumination on those areas which were white in the original document. International fax messages are transmitted by satellite.

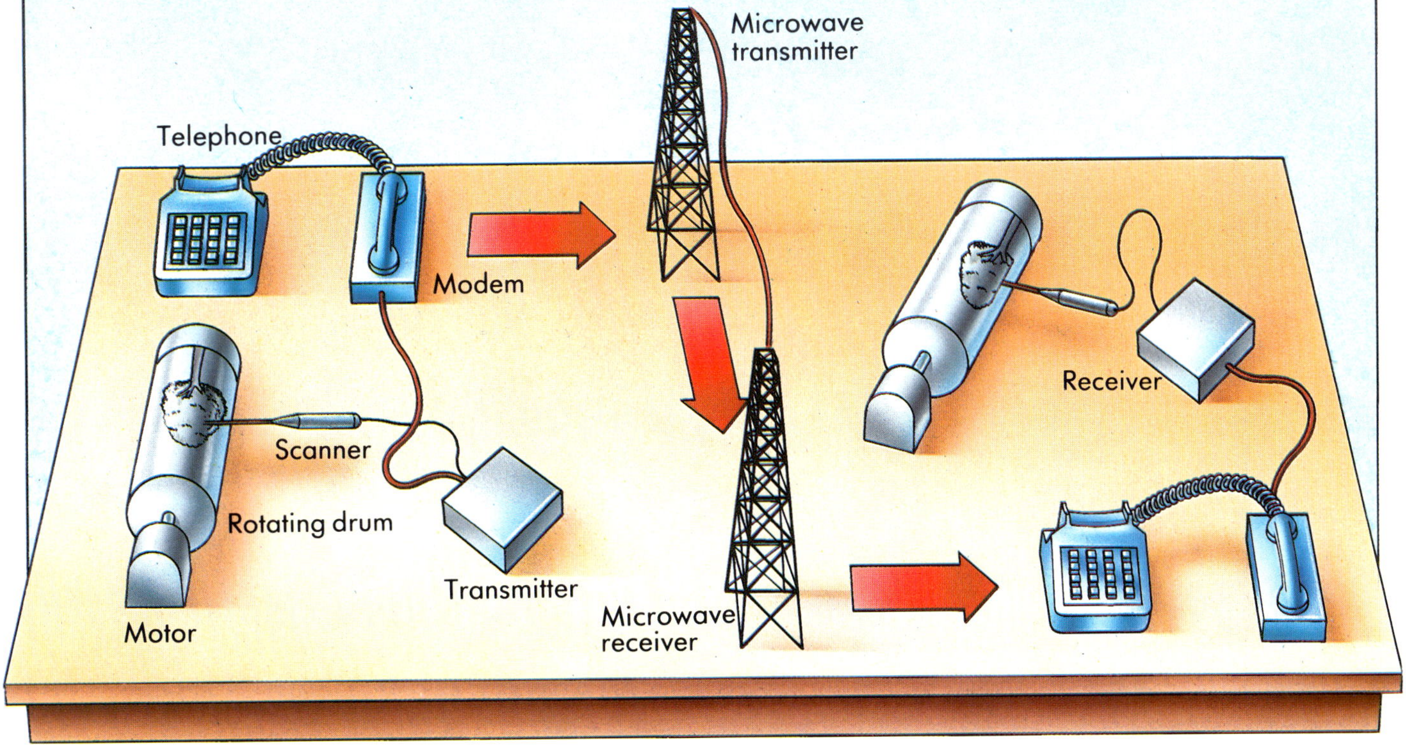

On the air

Spot facts

- *The first use of the radiomicrophone was in 1947. Reg Moores, an entertainer, used it in an ice-pantomime in Brighton, England.*
- *Up to 30 images, or 6,000 billion billion electrons, are normally transmitted by television every second. Images persist in the human eye for one-tenth of a second, so television must produce more than ten images per second to give the impression of a moving image.*
- *In the United States, any one television station uses as much space on the airwaves as all the AM radio channels put together.*
- *The first videophones appeared in the early 1970s. As the speaker's voice was relayed by telephone, his or her image was transmitted on a screen by closed-circuit television.*

Television and radio are the most used forms of mass communication. They are also the main source of entertainment in the home. Television and radio are broadcast from transmitters, which send their signals through the air in all directions. The signals can be picked up by an aerial attached to an individual set.

The advent of television has changed the view we have of the world, making it seem smaller. Live television broadcasts allow us to see events as they happen. We can watch momentous world events from the other side of the planet. We can have the best view in the sports stadium, and hear commentary on the game at the same time. Satellites which orbit the Earth at a height of over 35,000 km are used to relay television signals from distant places into our homes.

▶ The scene in a television broadcasting studio during the screening of the news and weather. A number of cameras are used to view the newscasters, who read from notes and from teleprompt screens.

Wireless telegraph

About one hundred years ago it was discovered that electric and magnetic energy could travel through the air, or even through empty space. This is called electromagnetic radiation. It was calculated that the speed at which this radiation should move was the same as the speed of light. It was realized that visible light is a kind of electromagnetic radiation, but that there are very many other kinds of electromagnetic radiation which are invisible to humans. These include what we now call gamma rays, X-rays, ultraviolet and infrared radiation, microwaves, and radio waves.

In all early forms of electrical communication, information was carried by an electric current travelling along a wire. Following the discovery of electromagnetic radiation, some people saw the possibility of using it to create a form of communication without wires. This wireless telegraph was developed in particular by an Italian called Guglielmo Marconi. His first working system used electric sparks to generate the electromagnetic radiation, and a coil of wire which could be attached to an earpiece to detect the radiation. The radio waves radiated from the spark in all directions. Some passed through the coil which generated a small current in the loop of wire. This was used to create a faint clicking sound in the earpiece.

Using this system, Marconi could send messages in Morse code between people who were not connected by a wire. In 1896 he sent Morse code messages for a short distance between a spark generator and a receiver. In 1901 he sent messages for nearly 5,000 km across the Atlantic Ocean. It surprised everybody that the radio waves could be received from so far away. It was later found that radio waves are reflected by the ionosphere and reach the Earth many thousands of kilometres away.

Electromagnetic waves

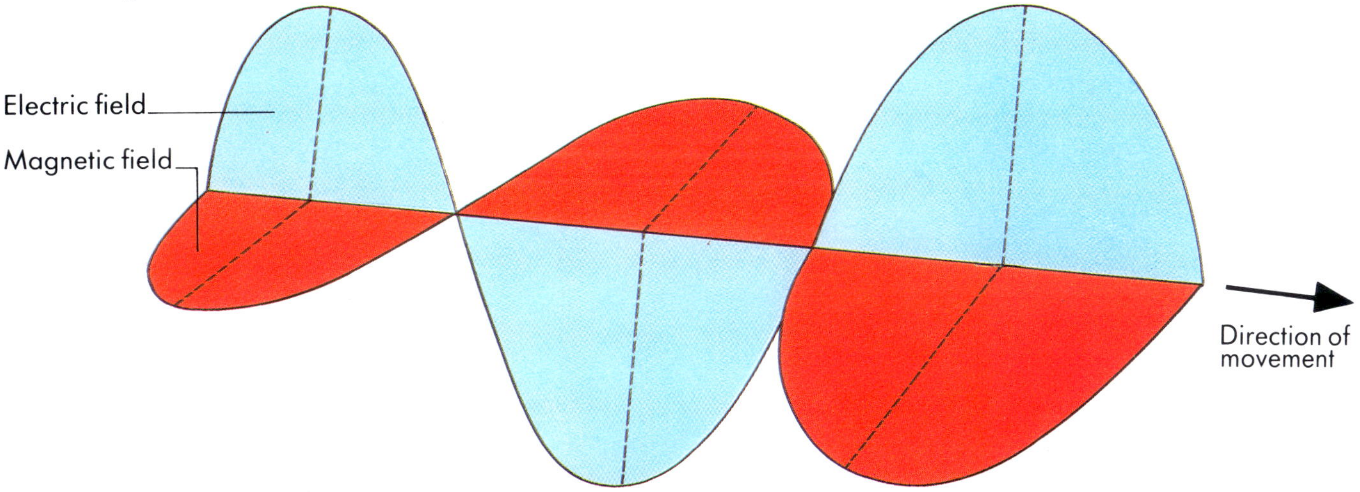

▲ Radio waves, X-rays, and visible light are all forms of electromagnetic radiation. The radiation consists of oscillating electric and magnetic fields which are at right-angles to each other. The waves can move through empty space. Electromagnetic radiation moves at just less than 300,000 km/sec.

◀ Guglielmo Marconi, who invented the first successful wireless telegraph. In 1901 he transmitted the Morse code signal for the letter S from Cornwall, England to Newfoundland, Canada across the Atlantic. He was awarded a Nobel prize in 1909.

Radio

Radio waves are a type of electromagnetic radiation. All electromagnetic radiation has a wavelength and a frequency. The wavelength is the distance between the peaks of the wave. The frequency is the number of times the wave goes up and down in a second. Wavelength is measured in metres; frequency is measured in hertz (Hz), kilohertz (kHz) or megahertz (mHz). A megahertz is a thousand kilohertz.

The first transatlantic radio messages of Marconi consisted of radiation at all frequencies which were sent in three short bursts to spell out the letter S in Morse code. With improvements in electronics at the beginning of the century, it became possible to produce radio waves at almost a single frequency. Radio receivers were also invented which could be tuned to detect a signal at a single frequency.

These two developments allow many radio stations to broadcast each on a different frequency for the listener to choose from. Radio broadcasts are made in three ranges of frequency. Long-wave signals have a frequency between 150 and 280 kHz. Medium waves lie between 540 and 1,600 kHz. The highest band, called FM, is between 88 and 108 MHz.

A radio system consists of a microphone linked to a transmitter, and a receiver linked to a loudspeaker. When someone speaks or plays music into the microphone, the sound waves are converted into electrical signals. These signals are then mixed with a radio wave. This is called modulation. The radio wave is called the carrier wave.

The radio wave with all the sound information on it is then beamed in all directions from high-power transmitters. A radio aerial can detect these radio waves passing across it. The aerial detects all frequencies but by tuning the radio to a particular position only one frequency is amplified within the radio. The radio subtracts the carrier wave from the signal which leaves the original sound information. This is used to drive a loudspeaker, which makes the sound from the radio audible.

▼ Radio signals controlling model aircraft. The joystick controls produce different signals depending on the direction of movement. The large aerial sends out the signal which is picked up by a receiver on the plane. This controls the movement of wings and rudder.

Modulation

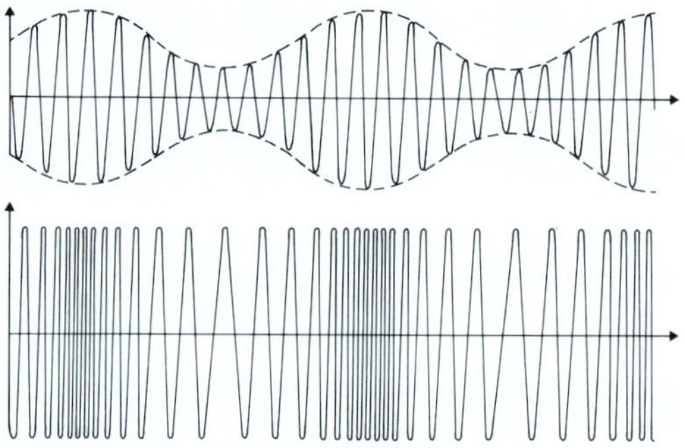

Modulation is the process of adding information on to a radio wave. A pure radio wave has a constant frequency and a constant signal strength (amplitude). It is possible either to change the amplitude of the carrier wave or to change its frequency to make it carry sound information to a radio receiver. These two methods are called amplitude modulation (AM) and frequency modulation (FM).

▲ Using a portable cellular telephone, a cross between a telephone handset and a "walkie-talkie" radio.

▶ In a cellular radio system, telephones link into the telephone network via local transmitters.

Cellular radio

▲ A local-radio DJ (disc jockey) speaks to a caller on a popular "phone-in" programme. Local-radio stations broadcast from FM transmitters, which have only a limited, above-the-horizon range.

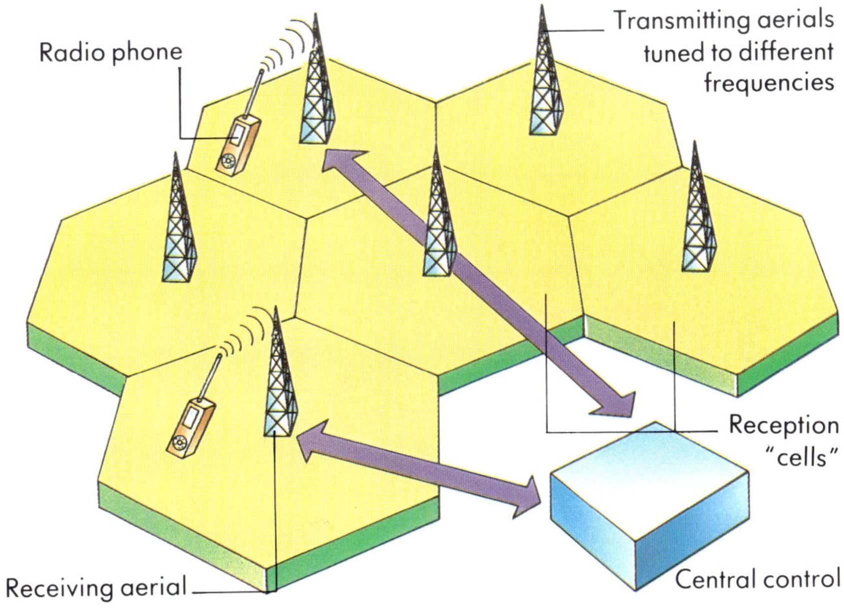

Television

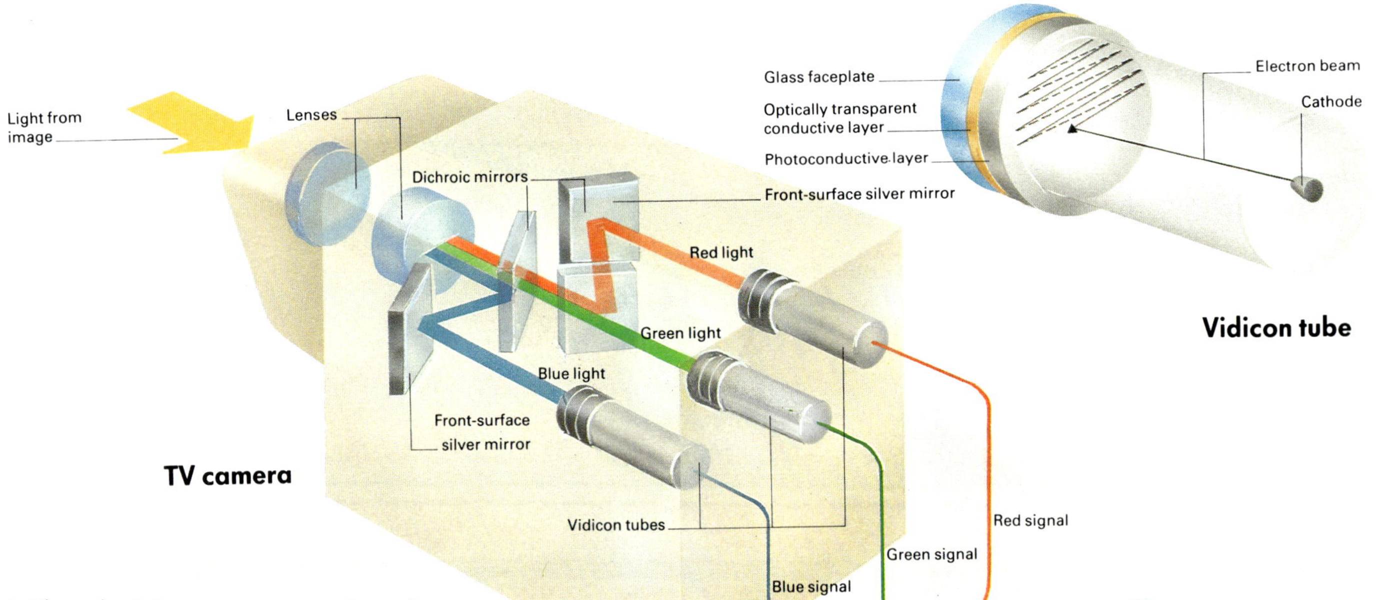

▲ The television camera consists of three detectors called vidicons. These detectors view the scene to be filmed through coloured filters. They react to the amount of red, green, or blue at each point in the scene. The light-sensitive surface of the vidicon is scanned by an electron beam, which can measure the amount of light that has hit the detector.

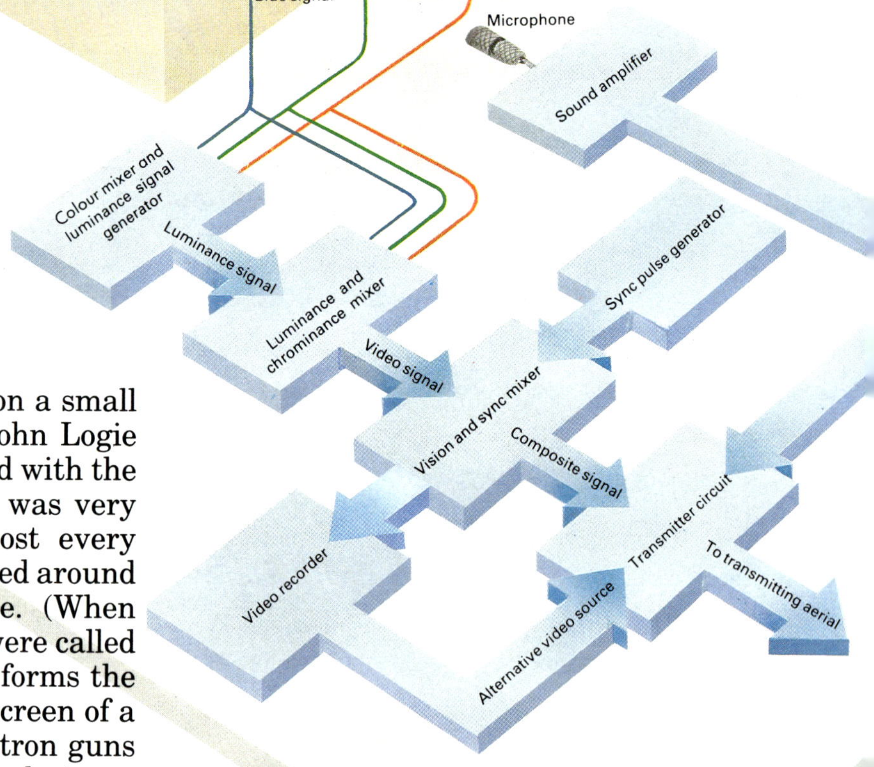

The first moving pictures appeared on a small screen in 1926. The inventor was John Logie Baird. Although he is usually credited with the invention of television, his machine was very different from those found in almost every house today. Modern television is based around a device called a cathode-ray tube. (When electrons were first discovered they were called cathode rays.) The front of the tube forms the screen of the television. Behind the screen of a colour television there are three electron guns which use a high voltage to speed up electrons and accelerate them towards the screen.

When electrons hit a point on the screen they make that position glow with a colour which depends on a chemical with which the screen is coated. A colour television screen is coated with three different chemicals (called phosphors) which glow red, green or blue. The picture is built up from dots or lines of only these colours. From a normal viewing distance these primary colours merge to reproduce the colour in the scene being televised. From close to the screen,

▲ The signals from each of the vidicon light detectors in the television camera are called the chrominance signals because they measure the amount of each colour. The signals are also used to measure the overall brightness of each part of the scene. This is the luminance signal. The chrominance and luminance signals are combined with the sound signal before being transmitted from the aerial.

the individual areas of primary colour are easily visible.

The screen is divided into many hundreds of horizontal lines of phosphors: 625 lines in the UK and Europe, 525 in the US and Japan. The electron beams are scanned across the screen, illuminating only a single point on the screen at any instant. The electrons are deflected by magnets, which scan the beam from left to right across the first line. The beam then jumps back across the screen and scans the third line, also from left to right. The scanning continues on every other line until the bottom of the screen is reached. This takes one-fiftieth of a second. The beam then jumps back to the second line and fills in the even-numbered lines in the same way. A complete screen is drawn in one twenty-fifth of a second. This scanning rate of twenty-five frames a second is enough for the scanning to be invisible to the human eye.

▼ The signal is picked up by the aerial. It is passed into the TV set where it is split into its constituent parts. The sound signal goes to the loudspeaker. The luminance and chrominance information goes to the electron guns, which illuminate the phosphors on the screen so as to produce a colour image of the scene as viewed by the camera.

▼ The three electron beams are fired towards the screen. The screen is coated with lines of blue, green and red phosphors which glow with colour when they are energized by the electrons.

TV receiver

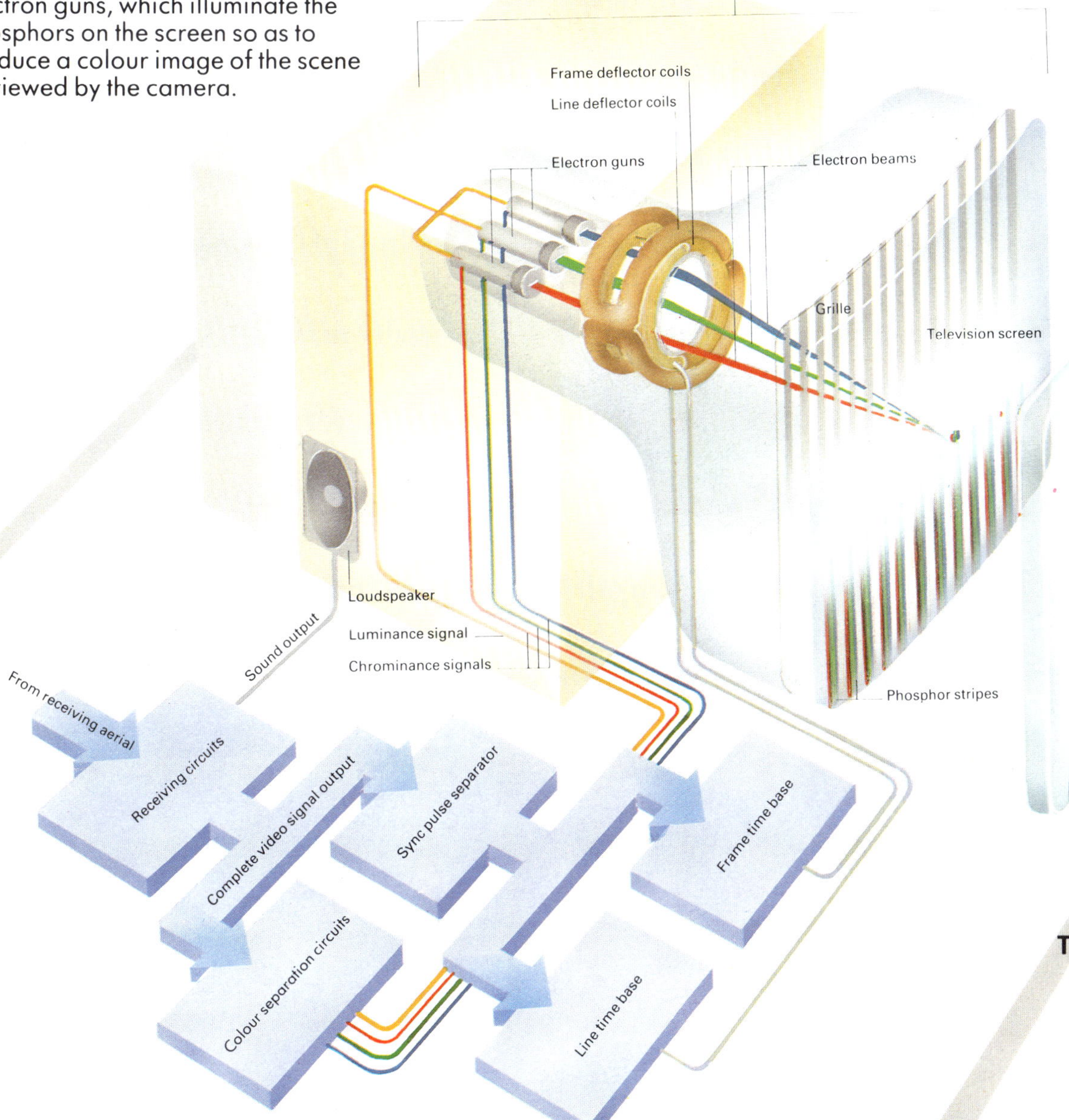

Trinitron screen

On screen

Television is an extremely popular source of entertainment and information. In Western Europe there is a television in most homes. In the United States there are almost as many televisions as there are people in the country. The widespread ownership of television sets and the enthusiasm of people to watch them make broadcasting on television a very efficient way of reaching the attention of millions of viewers. Companies pay large amounts of money to advertise their products in breaks during and between programmes.

In most countries the broadcasting organizations are separate from the government, and many are independent companies. By transmitting their programmes on cable networks or via satellite, they provide many different channels.

A television aerial will pick up programmes sent through the air from powerful transmitting towers. Television programmes can also arrive in the home along cables or from a satellite. In a cable TV network, a wire runs from each house to a main cable. The main cable is connected to either a local receiving antenna or directly to the television station. Cable TV became widespread in cities in the United States, where the many tall steel buildings make conventional TV reception difficult.

Television signals can also be transmitted from the TV station to one of the communication satellites that orbit the Earth. The satellite receives the transmissions and sends them back to Earth, radiating the signal over a large area of land. The programmes are picked up by means of a small dish aerial.

In addition to broadcasting programmes, television can display pages of information. The information is sent by the TV company but the TV owner has to install an electronic unit which decodes the signal and displays the text. A similar system called Viewdata allows the TV user access to large banks of information via a telephone line. The databank can be questioned and the answer displayed on the screen.

Cable television

People who subscribe to a cable-TV network watch television programmes received, not via an external aerial, but via cable. The network control station (picture right) receives programmes beamed down to it from one or more communications satellites.

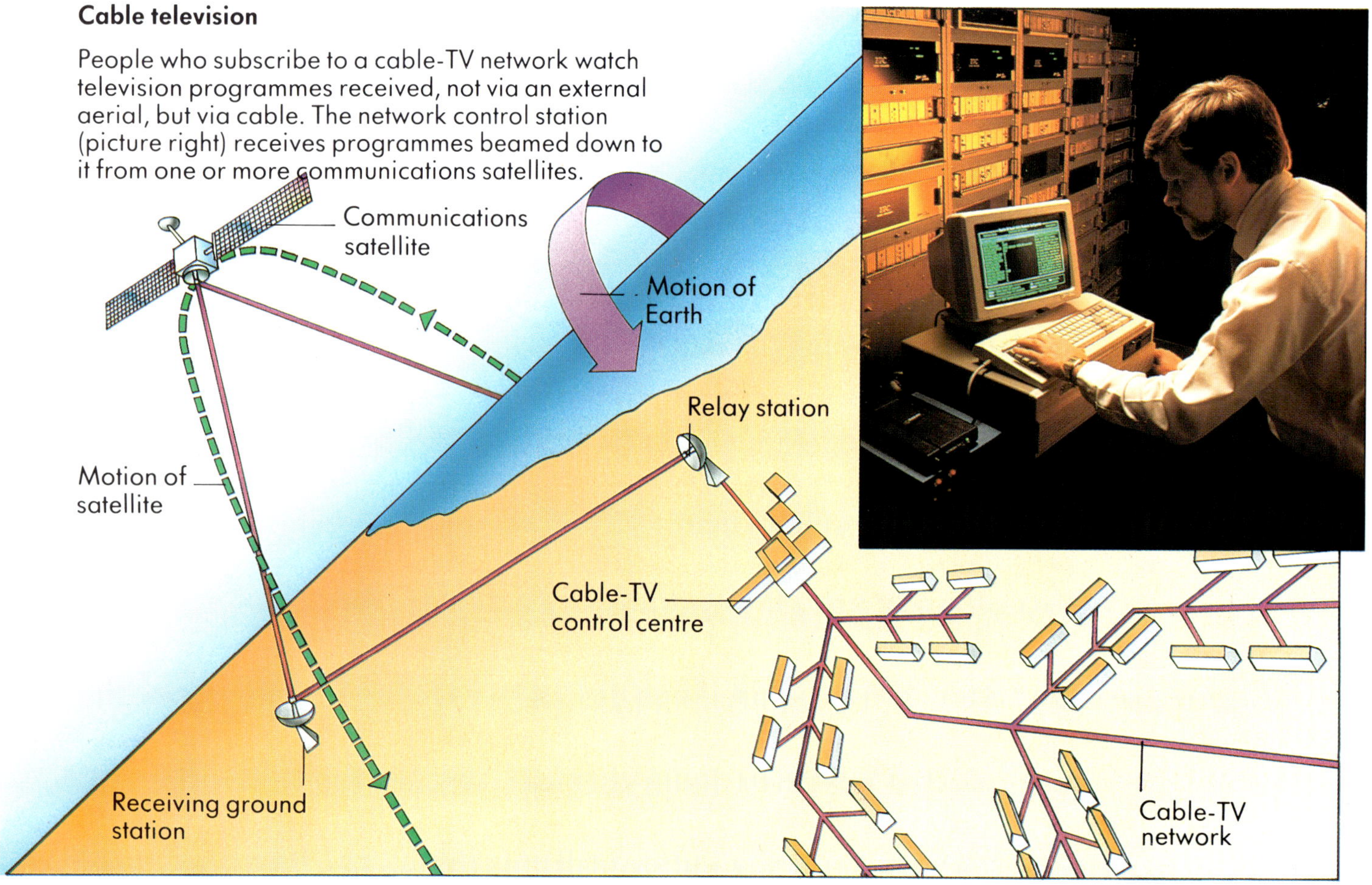

▲ A watch-TV, which uses liquid crystal display (LCD) to create a black-and-white picture. The screen is made up of liquid-crystal cells, which change their reflectivity when an electric field is applied to them. Other new technologies are leading to the development of full-size flat-screen TV receivers.

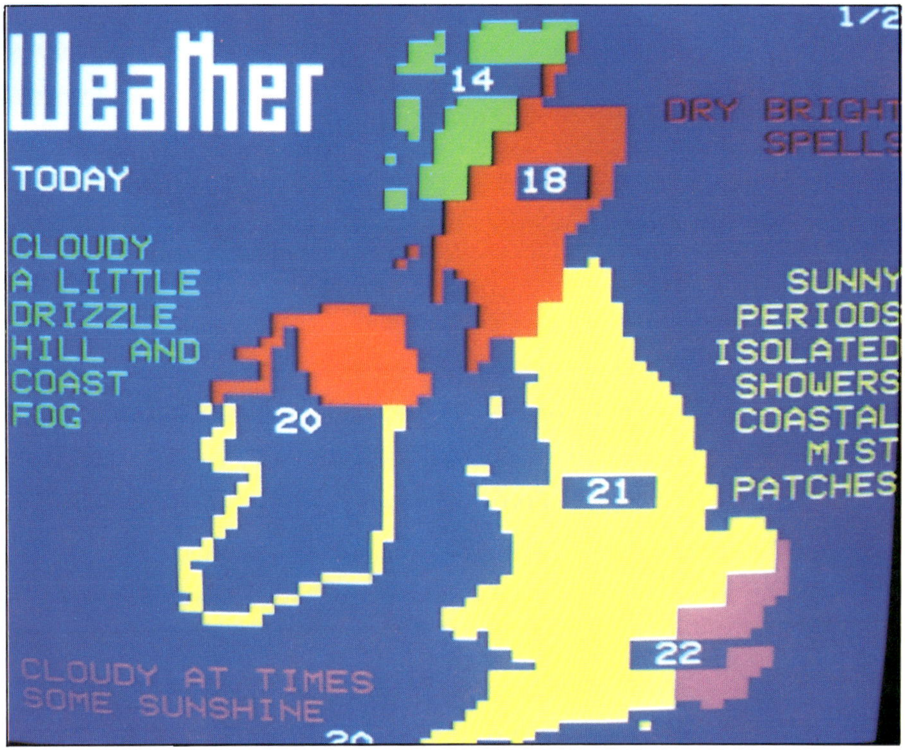

▲ The weather "page" of the Ceefax information "magazine" broadcast on television by the British Broadcasting Corporation (BBC). The BBC pioneered the system, called teletext, in the 1970s.

▼ Closed-circuit television (CCTV) being used at the Live Aid pop concert in London in 1985 to give the audience a better view of the performers. The concert was also relayed worldwide by satellite.

Recording

Sound can be recorded and replayed in many different ways. The methods which are in everyday use are magnetic tape, record and compact disc. To record on tape, the sound is converted to electric signals, which are used to alter the magnetism of the tape. To manufacture a record, the sound vibrations are fed to a cutter, which makes a wavy groove in a plastic disc. For the compact disc the sound is converted to a string of numbers, which represent the sound waves. The numbers are recorded on the disc and "read" by laser.

The more difficult problem of recording picture information can also be solved using either magnetic tape (video) or compact disc. The main use of these inventions is in home entertainment and in broadcasting.

Spot facts

- *The nursery rhyme "Mary had a little lamb" was the first sound recording played in public in 1877. The reciter was the US inventor Thomas A. Edison, who recorded and played it back on his "favorite invention", the phonograph.*
- *Early phonographs used cactus needles for styli. The tip radius of the stylus of old 78 rpm record players was 0.007 cm. The modern playback stylus has a tip radius of 0.0005 cm.*
- *Modern manufacturing techniques can produce long-playing discs with a surface accuracy of more than 0.00025 cm.*
- *A compact disc can still reproduce music perfectly, even when it has a hole drilled through it.*

► Young people gyrate to the throbbing music at a discotheque in Disneyland, Los Angeles, USA. Disco dancing to records remains as popular as ever. But for personal listening, cassette tapes are now preferred.

Microphones and speakers

Sound waves are a variation in air pressure. Microphones have to use this varying air pressure to produce a similar variation in a voltage or current within the microphone. In that way, electrical signals can be sent along wires from the microphone. There are two main types of microphone in use today. One is the dynamic microphone, the other is the condenser microphone. Both types have a thin sheet, or diaphragm, behind a protective front cover.

In the dynamic microphone, there is a coil of wire attached behind the diaphragm. A movement of the diaphragm in response to the varying air pressure of sound waves also moves the coil past a magnet in the microphone. This creates a varying electric current in the coil. In the condenser microphone, the diaphragm movement changes the spacing between it and a second sheet positioned behind it. This changes an electrical property called capacitance. As the capacitance changes, electric current travels along the wires from the microphone.

▼ Microphones convert the pressure variations of the sound waves into similar variations in electric current. The movement of the diaphragm changes the distance between the diaphragm and a charged plate. This changes the amount of charge the plate can hold as provided by the battery. As it changes, current is moved along the wires from the microphone.

Microphone

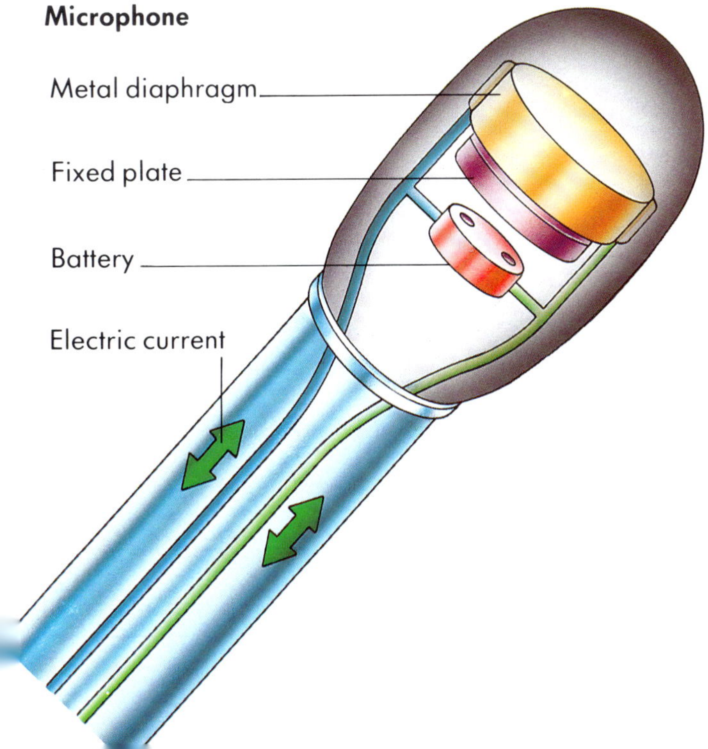

Loudspeakers

Loudspeakers have to convert a varying electrical signal into sound. They do this by using the signal to move of the thin cone which forms the front of the speaker. The movement sets up air pressure variations, which reproduce the original sound. The most common design of speaker operates in a similar way to the dynamic microphone. A coil of wire, which is attached to the speaker cone, sits in the field of a magnet. The electric signal is fed into the coil which causes it to move in the magnetic field. This makes the speaker cone vibrate to match the oscillations of the electric current.

To reproduce accurately the original sounds, it is important to have a range of speakers of different physical size. Small speakers (called tweeters) are good for reproducing high-pitched sounds. Large speakers (called woofers) are best for low-pitched sounds. The accuracy of sound reproduction is called fidelity. Very high fidelity (hi-fi) speakers have three cones, each for a different frequency range.

Loudspeaker

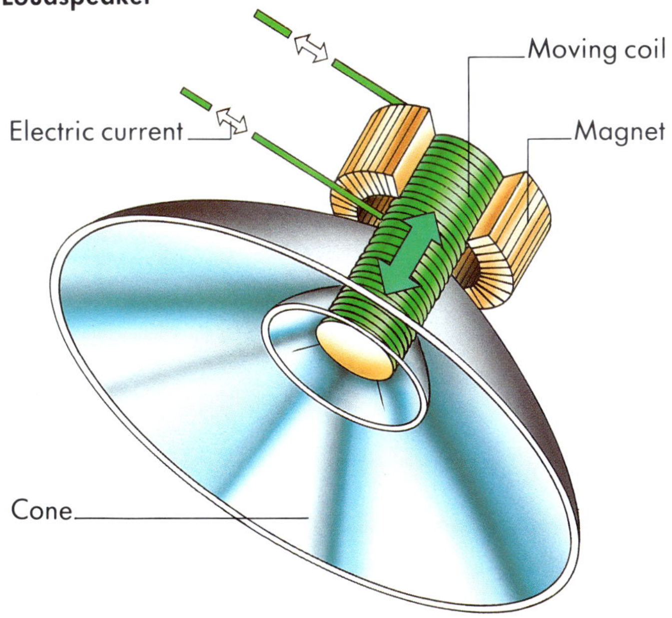

▲ When the varying electric current reaches the loudspeaker, it is fed to a coil. The coil sits in a magnetic field. Changes in the current alter the amount of force which the magnetic field exerts on the coil. The coil moves backwards and forwards inside the magnet. The coil is attached to a thin paper cone. The cone moves the air around it to reproduce the pressure variations in the original sounds.

Disc and tape

Sound can be permanently recorded and played back using either magnetic tape (reel-to-reel and cassette) or plastic discs (records). To record on a magnetic tape, the electric signal from a microphone is fed to an electromagnet which forms the main part of the recording head of a tape recorder. The tape is drawn past the recording head as it is wound from one spool to the other. It is very important that this movement is smooth. When playing back the tape, it has to move at the same speed as that of the recording. The tape has a thin layer of tiny metallic crystals of iron oxide. Each one of the crystals can act as a magnet. When the tape passes over the recording head, the crystals are magnetized so that the poles point in a particular direction. When the tape is played back the process is reversed. The magnetization of the crystals induces currents in the replay head, which are passed to a loudspeaker to reproduce the original sounds.

Recording on magnetic tape is also the first step in making a recording on disc. The taped sounds are fed to a cutter which scores a groove in the disc. The waviness of the groove contains the information about the volume and pitch of the original sounds. This first disc is then used to produce a metal copy. The metal copy has ridges which exactly match the grooves in the

▼ A recent very successful development in tape technology is the personal stereo, often called a walkman. Great effort was invested by many Japanese companies, particularly Sony, in the miniaturization of the tape player and in the design and appearance of the product.

The pioneers

Towards the end of the 1800s two systems of sound reproduction were invented. The reel-to-reel system, invented by Valdemar Poulsen, stored sound on a magnetized steel wire. The wax cylinder system was invented by Thomas Edison (right). It stored sound in grooves in the wax.

original plastic (acetate) disc. Two metal copies are required, one for each side of the record. To produce a record, blank plastic discs are pressed between the two metal masters. This produces a groove in each side of the disc, which is a copy of the original. When the stylus of the record player runs in the groove, its vibrations are picked up and translated into electrical signals. The signals are amplified and fed to the speakers of the system.

To make a stereo recording on a disc, the groove is produced by two cutters. Each cutter forms the shape of one side of the valley of the groove. When the disc is played, the effect on the stylus from the two differently-shaped sides of the groove can be split up in the stylus cartridge. Two signals are sent from the pick-up arm to the amplifier. The amplified signals are then sent to separate loudspeakers, which together reproduce stereophonic sounds.

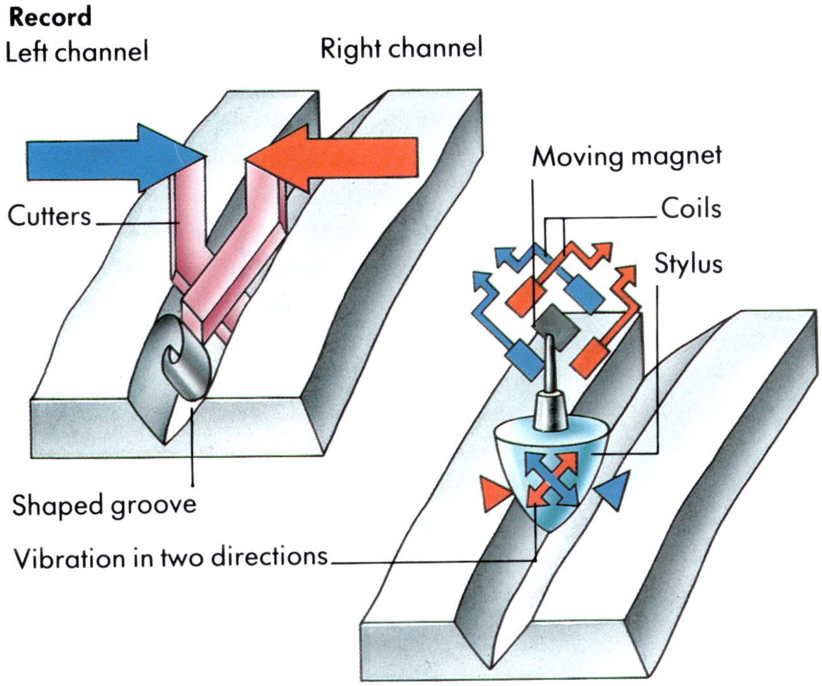

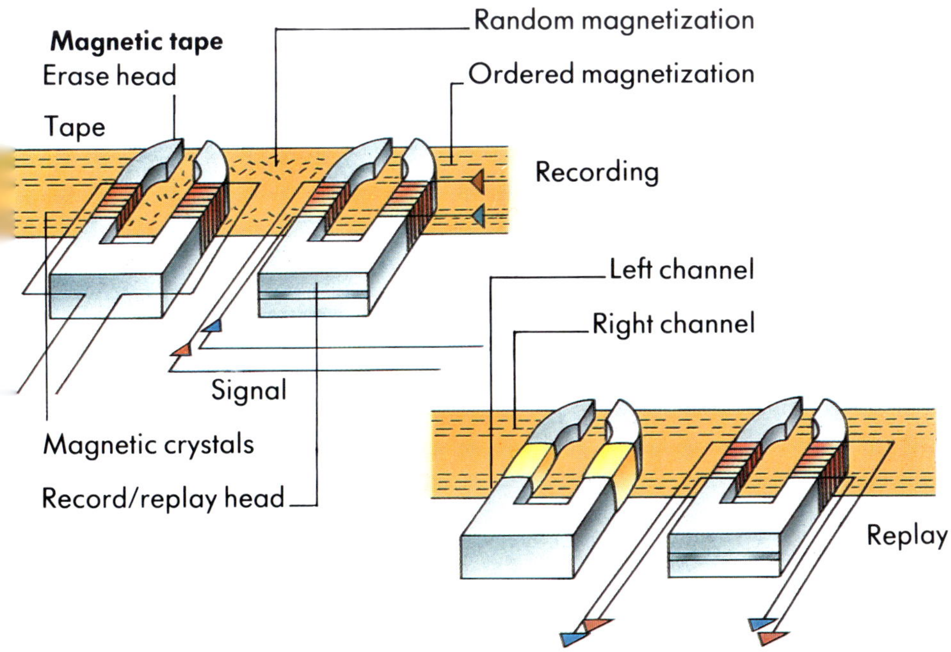

◄▲ Sound is stored on plastic discs in the shape of the groove which is cut in the disc. The original sound is fed to cutters, which shape a long spiral groove in a disc of acetate. Stereo sound is reproduced by cutting the two sides of the groove with different shapes. The sound is reproduced by a diamond stylus (photo above) which runs in the groove and vibrates as it is moved by the wavy edges. Sound is stored on tape in the magnetism of a thin layer of iron oxide crystals which coat the plastic tape. Varying currents from a microphone change the strength of the magnetic field of the recording head. This magnetizes the crystals in particular directions. Running the tape past the replay head induces electric currents, which are fed to a loudspeaker. Stereo recordings can also be made on magnetic tape. The recording is made in two tracks at different positions across the tape. The sounds on each track are played back through loudspeakers.

Video

Television pictures can be stored on videotape in the same way that sound can be recorded on audio tape. The two kinds of tape are made from similar material: magnetized iron oxide particles on a plastic tape. But vastly more information has to be put on the video tape than on the audio cassette. Twenty-five times every second the video recording head has to put information on to the tape. This information is on the brightness and colour at each point of the 625 lines of the television screen.

The first video machines which used magnetic tape tried to use exactly the same recording technique as an audio tape recorder. The recording head was kept stationary and the tape was moved past it. Because of the enormous amount of information that had to be recorded, the tape had to be moved extremely quickly over the head. Speeds of up to ten metres per second were used. Modern video recorders move the tape at only two centimetres per second, five hundred times slower. The decrease in speed has been made possible by very great improvements in the way that television picture information is put on to the tape by the recording head.

Modern video recorders
Instead of moving the tape very quickly past the head, modern video recorders move the head very quickly past the tape by fixing it to a cylinder which is rotated at high speed. When a videotape is put into a video cassette recorder (VCR), the cover that protects the tape is lifted and two plastic posts rise behind the tape and pull it out of the cassette. The tape is wrapped around the recording head cylinder. The cylinder contains two recording/play heads which rotate with it. The cylinder is twice as wide as the tape and set at an angle to it. As the cylinder rotates beneath the angled tape, the recording heads write the information on the tape in long diagonal lines, which run from one edge of the tape to the other.

There are two main VCR systems: Betamax and VHS (Video Home System). Both use 19-mm wide tape.

▼ The use of a video camera recorder (camcorder) for recording family events and holidays is becoming more and more popular. Simple camcorders are available now which record picture and sound at the same time. Tapes recorded like this can be played back on standard VCR machines.

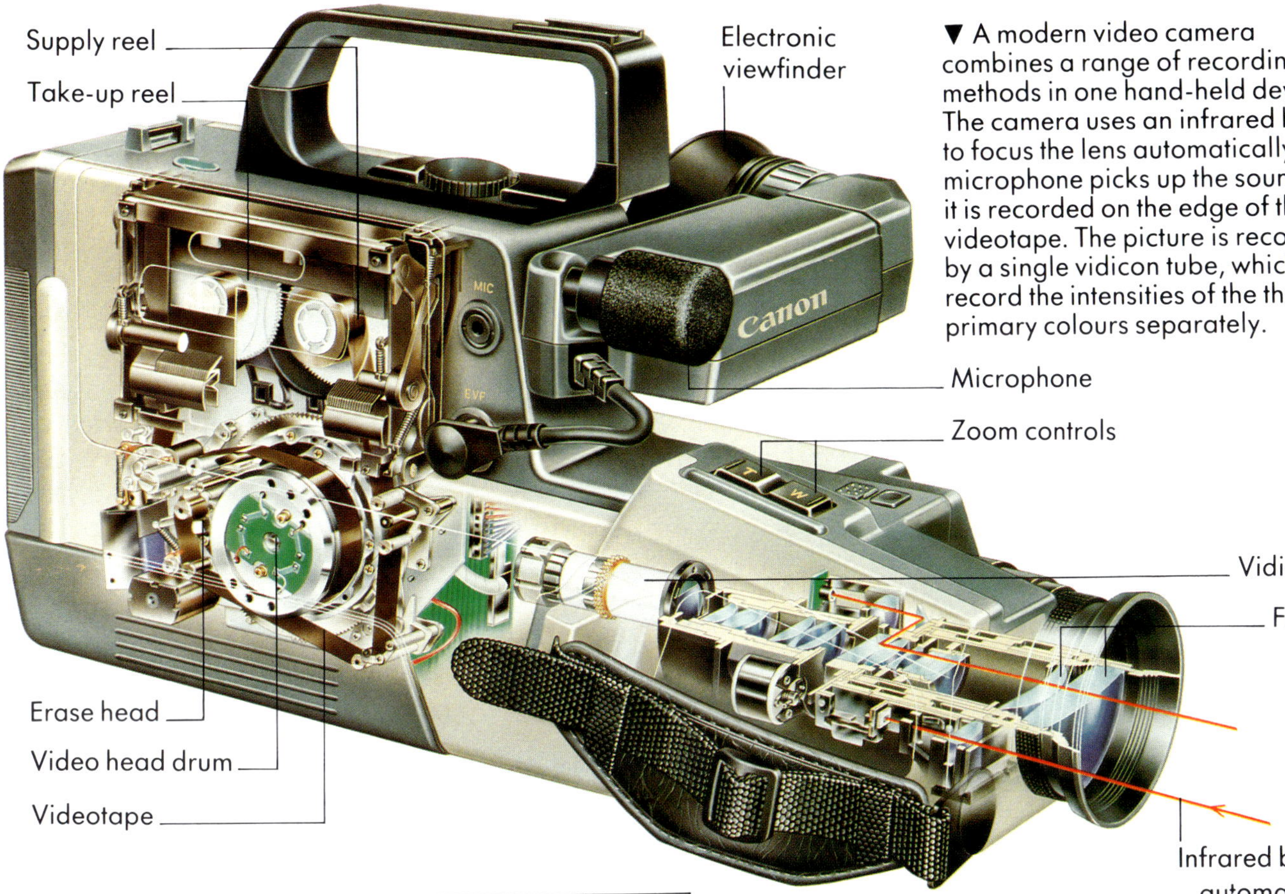

▼ A modern video camera combines a range of recording methods in one hand-held device. The camera uses an infrared beam to focus the lens automatically. The microphone picks up the sound and it is recorded on the edge of the videotape. The picture is recorded by a single vidicon tube, which can record the intensities of the three primary colours separately.

Videotape recording

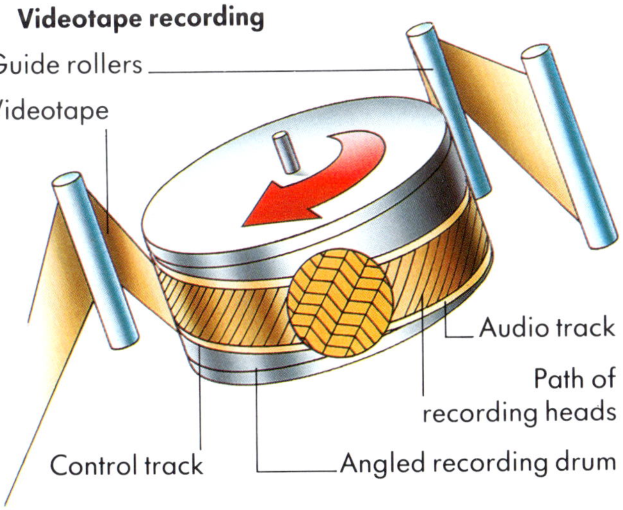

Two recording heads are positioned on the rotating cylinder. As they pass the tape they write diagonally across it because of the angle of the cylinder. Because of the different angles at which the recording heads are set, each head cannot read information from the tracks on either side. This reduces interference and allows more room for information on the tape.

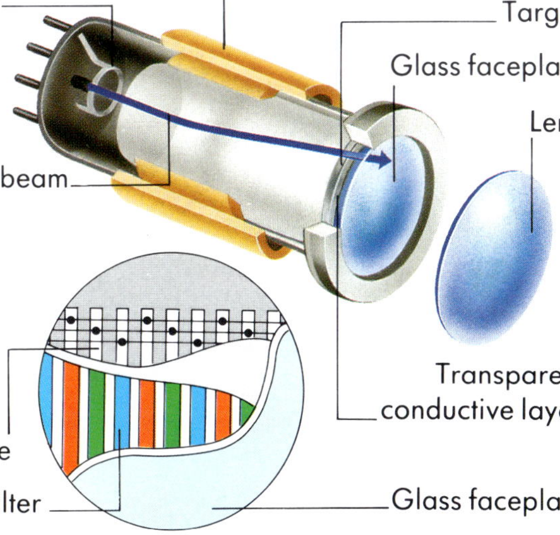

▲ This is a single vidicon tube which can measure the brightness of each of the colours red, green and blue. Behind the glass plate at the front, there is an array of very small filters which allow through only one of the colours. Behind the filter the electron beam can measure separately the light intensity of each colour.

Digital discs

The newest form of recording to reach the home is the compact disc. The discs themselves and the disc players require very precise and controlled manufacturing methods. This makes them probably the most complicated and advanced machines that are in everyday use in the home.

There are three main features of compact discs which make the quality of the sound obtainable from them superior. The first is that sound is recorded digitally on them, and played back digitally. The second is that unlike the stylus of a record player, or the recording head of a tape recorder, the device used to "read" the sound does not actually touch the disc. This removes the danger of damage to the disc and even prevents the usual wear and tear. The third is that sound is recorded more than once on the disc. These features combine to improve the sound quality and the lifetime of the disc.

▼ A compact disc is 120 mm in diameter and 1.2 mm thick. It can store up to 74 minutes of music. A close-up of the surface of the disc (on the right) shows the pattern of pits which store the sounds.

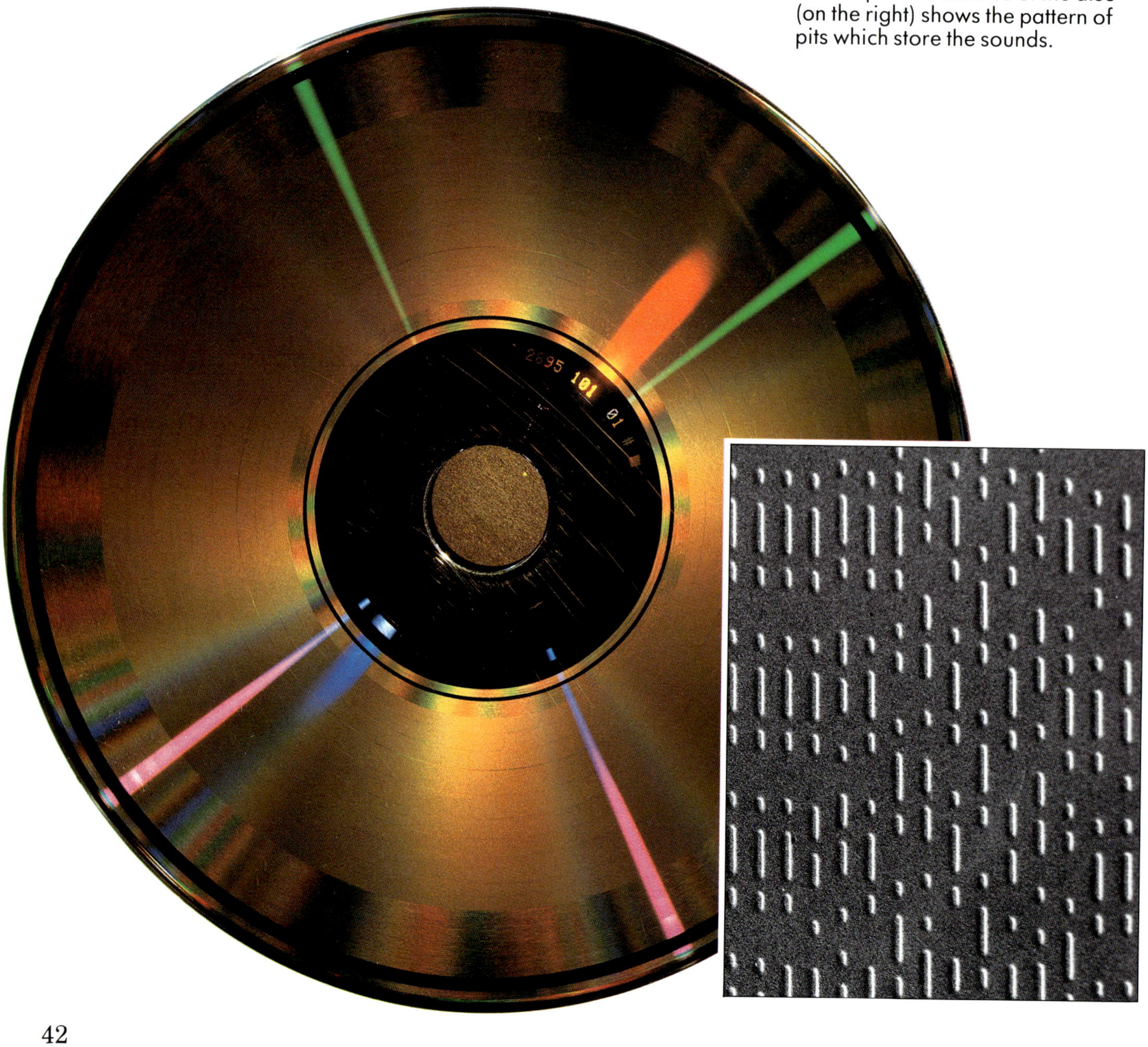

In digital recording, the sound is not recorded as the depth of a groove nor the magnetization of a tape. Its intensity is converted into a binary number and this number is put on to the disc. All the zeros in the number are represented by small pits in the disc.

Reading by laser

As a laser scans the disc, its light is reflected efficiently by the smooth surface of the disc but is scattered in all directions when it strikes a pit in the surface. By measuring changes in the brightness of the reflected light, the disc player can read the lines of zeros or ones that represent the sound intensity values. By converting these intensities to electrical signals which drive a loudspeaker, the original sound is read from the disc and reproduced so that it can be heard.

The laser beam is scanned in a spiral beneath the disc by a pair of mirrors. The beam is focused on the recorded surface through the plastic cover of the disc. Lasers are used because they are very bright and can be focused on to very small spots.

To reduce the likelihood of making a mistake in reading the disc, the sound values are recorded several times on the disc. All the recordings are read by the laser and compared with each other. If one reading is different from the others because of a scratch or mistake in the manufacture, that particular reading is not sent to the loudspeaker.

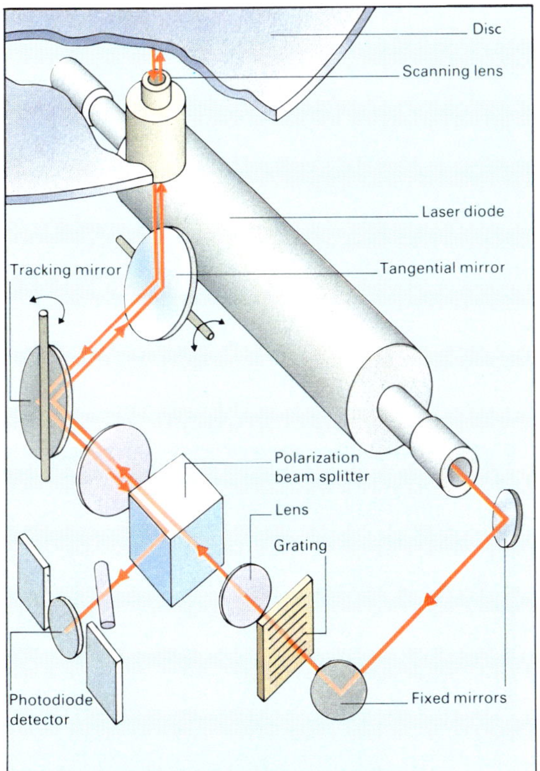

Reading from a compact disc

An array of mirrors transmits the laser beam to a scanning lens which focuses the laser light on to the underside of the disc. As the disc rotates, the lens moves to follow the spiral track of sound information. The mirrors also move to keep the beam pointed at the lens.

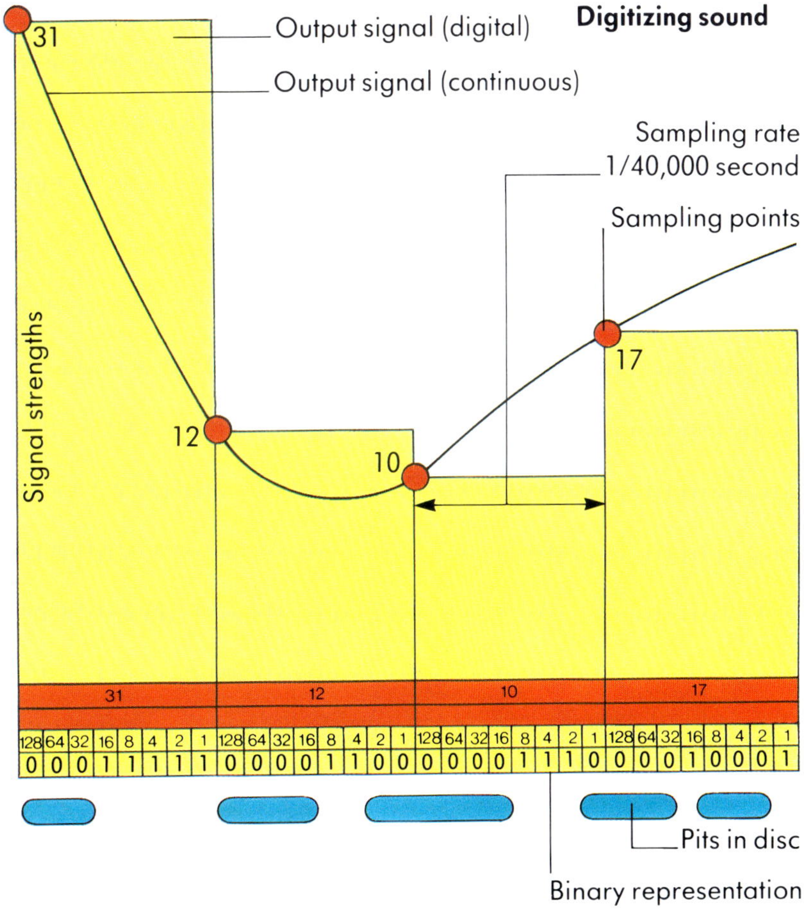

▲ Digitization of a sound signal involves measuring the intensity of the sound at regular intervals. Measurements are taken 40,000 times every second. Each value of sound intensity is converted into a binary number, a string of zeros and ones. These numbers are recorded on the disc by cutting small pits in the disc to represent a zero or a line of zeros.

Glossary

aerial An electrically-conducting device which can intercept radio or television waves in the air and pass them to an amplifier and loudspeaker.

air pressure The density of air molecules at a particular point in space. Sound waves are variations in air pressure which move through the air.

AM (Amplitude Modulation) A system of carrying sound signals on a radio wave by varying the amplitude (height) of the radio wave.

aperture The hole behind the lens of a camera which allows light to fall on to the film. Decreasing the size of the aperture increases the depth of field but also increases the required exposure time.

bandwidth A range of frequencies. The range required to carry the information for a radio, telephone, or television signal.

binary The binary numbering system uses only ones and zeros to express a number. Instead of columns for units, tens, hundreds, etc. the binary system uses columns for units, twos, fours, eights, sixteens, and so on.

camcorder The name sometimes given to a camera which records onto a video cassette. The name is a shortening of "camera recorder".

capacitor A device for storing electrical charge.

carrier frequency The fundamental frequency of the electromagnetic wave which is used to carry a radio, telephone or television signal through the air.

cathode A negatively-charged electrode. The positive electrode is the anode. Electrons will flow from the cathode to the anode.

cathode-ray tube The central component of a television. A beam of electrons is directed towards a screen where a chemical coating gives off light at the point which the beam hits. The beam direction can be rapidly changed by varying the voltage on electrodes on each side of the electron beam.

cellular radio Also called cellular phone. A local communication system in which each small area or cell is served by its own transmitter. Communications between cells go via a central control computer.

chrominance signal The information on how much of each of the colours red, green and blue should be shown on each point of a TV screen.

compact disc An information storage system which may replace magnetic tape in many applications. The information is stored in binary code and is read from the surface of the disc by a laser.

complementary colour A colour and its complementary colour are opposite to each other. When the two are added the result is either black (in printing or photography) or white (in a TV).

contact prints A print made by placing a negative on a piece of film and then exposing the film to light through the negative.

daguerreotype One of the first types of photograph. It did not use film but exposed a picture on to a metal plate.

depth of field The range of distances from the camera which are brought into focus by the camera lens at one time. The depth of field is determined by the aperture size.

diaphragm A thin sheet of material which moves in response to variations in air pressure in a sound wave.

dichroic mirrors Mirrors which reflect some colours of light and transmit other colours. They are used to separate colours.

digital information Information expressed as a series of numbers.

electromagnetic radiation Radiation which consists of oscillating electric and magnetic fields. This includes radio, X-rays, and visible light. Unlike sound which needs air or another substance through which to travel, electromagnetic radiation can travel across completely empty space.

electron A negatively-charged particle. The movement of electrons constitutes an electric current. Electrons are also a constituent of atoms.

exposure time The length of time for which the shutter on a camera is opened. With a longer exposure time, more light will reach the film.

focusing Adjusting a lens so that the image formed by the lens is as sharp and clear as possible.

FM (Frequency Modulation) A system of carrying sound signals on a radio wave by varying the frequency of the radio wave.

frequency The frequency of a wave describes how many times it goes up and down in a second. Frequency is measured in hertz (Hz). One hertz is one oscillation per second.

galley A metal tray into which completed lines of typeset material are placed. When the page is complete, the galley is used to print from. This print is called the galley proof.

geostationary At a constant position above a particular point on the Earth's surface. Geostationary satellites have to be above the Equator and at a set distance (36,000 km) from the Earth. This is one-tenth of the distance to the Moon.

gravure A method of printing in which the printing plate contains many thousands of small indentations which hold the ink.

hertz (Hz) The unit of frequency. One hertz is one oscillation per second. Sound waves are measured in hertz or kilohertz (one thousand hertz). Radio waves are in the range 100 kHz to 100 MHz. One megahertz (MHz) is one million hertz. Visible light frequencies are about 100 million megahertz.

infrared radiation Electromagnetic radiation having a wavelength longer than visible light but shorter than microwaves. Wavelengths in the range 0.7 micron to 0.1 mm.

ionosphere Layers of the atmosphere which contain charged particles. They lie at a height of between 50 km and 500 km. The ionosphere is used to reflect radio waves back to Earth.

laser A device which can produce extremely intense, highly focusable beams of electromagnetic radiation. Most lasers give out visible light or infrared radiation.

letterpress A method of printing in which the area to be printed is raised above the background. The raised surface is inked and paper is pressed against it.

luminance signal The information on the overall brightness of each point to be shown on a TV screen.

micron A unit of length. One millionth of a meter.

microwaves Electromagnetic radiation having a wavelength longer than infrared radiation but shorter than radio waves. Wavelengths in the range 0.1 mm to 1 m.

modem (modulator-demodulator) A device which takes digital information and modifies it so that the information can be sent along a telephone line. At the other end of the line a second modem will extract from the signal the original information, presented as either words or pictures.

modulation The alteration of either the frequency or the amplitude of a wave.

movable type The printing technique of setting a page of type by putting together separate metal letters to copy the page to be printed.

multiplexing Using a single cable to carry more than one signal at a time.

negative A photograph in which the areas of light and dark are reversed. A bright area in the photographed scene produces a dark area on the negative. Colour negatives contain the complementary colour of the scene.

optical fibre A thin strand of transparent material contained in a plastic sleeve. Light can pass along the fibre without being lost from the sides.

oscillation The oscillation of a wave is the increase and decrease of whatever the wave is made of. For a sound wave it is the air pressure which oscillates. For a light wave it is the electric and magnetic fields.

pentaprism A five-sided piece of glass positioned behind the viewfinder in a camera.

phosphor A chemical coating on a TV screen which gives off red, green or blue light when it is hit by an electron beam.

photoconductive material A material which changes its ability to conduct electricity when it is exposed to light.

positive A photograph in which brightness and colour are the same as in the photographed scene.

primary colours A set of colours from which all other colours may be produced. In painting and printing, the primary colours are red, yellow and blue. In television, the primary colours are red, green and blue.

radio waves Electromagnetic radiation having a wavelength longer than microwaves. Wavelengths greater than 1 m.

resistance A property of all materials which measures how well they conduct electricity.

satellite A relay station in space which detects, amplifies and retransmits communications between distant points on Earth.

screening The process of changing an original photograph into one composed of millions of dots.

silver halide The light-sensitive material in photographic film. The crystals of silver halide darken when they are exposed to light.

stylus A sharp needle, usually of synthetic diamond, used to detect the shape of the groove in a record.

sync (synchronization) A timing pulse which is sent with a TV signal to ensure that the brightness, colour and sound information for each frame are kept together.

telegraph The long-distance transmission of simple information such as the dots and dashes of Morse code, or the movement of magnetic needles.

transducer A device which measures a physical property such as air pressure and converts the measurements into an electrical signal.

VHF/UHF/SHF Frequency ranges of radio waves: Very High Frequency, Ultra High Frequency, Super High Frequency.

vidicon A detector which measures the brightness at each point of an image focused on to its surface.

wavelength The distance between successive peaks in a wave. Radio waves have a wavelength between a few metres and a few kilometres. Visible light has a wavelength of less than one-millionth of a metre.

Index

Page numbers in *italics* refer to pictures.

Further Reading

Alexander Graham Bell by Andrew Dunn (Wayland, 1990)
Camera Technology by Alastair Jervis (Wayland, 1990)
Collins Guide to Modern Technology by Robin Kerrod (Collins, 1983)
Encyclopedia of Modern Technology by D. Blackburn and G. Holister (ed.) (Hutchinson, 1987)
Guglielmo Marconi by Nina Morgan (Wayland, 1990)
The Media: Radio by Rebecca Coyle (Wayland, 1988)
Messages on the Move; *Space Talk*; and *Sound and Vision* (Dataworld series) by Robin Kerrod (Granada, 1986)
Photography by David Cumming (Wayland, 1989)
Sound Systems by D. Aldous (Kingfisher, 1983)
Television by F. Wheen (Century Publishing, 1985)
Television and Video by H. Mintern (Kingfisher, 1983)
TV and Video Technology by Mark Lambert (Wayland, 1989)

Picture Credits

b=bottom, t=top, c=centre, l=left, r=right.

MH Michael Holford, Essex. NHPA Natural History Photographic Agency, Sussex. PP Picturepoint Ltd, Surrey. RF Rex Features, London. SCL Spectrum Colour Library, London. SPL Science Photo Library, London.

4 Zefa/Ted Horowtiz. 6 The Ridgeway Archive. 7l RF. 7r, 8, 9 Zefa. 10l Mary Evans Picture Library. 10r Art Directors. 12 SCL/Muhlberger. 13l Bayerisches National Museum. 13r Ann Ronan Picture Library. 14 Kodak. 17t MH/Science Museum. 17b Minolta. 18l NHPA/S Dalton. 18r SPL. 19 PP. 20 Sally & Richard Greenhill. 21l, 21r MH/Science Museum. 22l British Telecom. 22r Telefocus. 24 AT&T. 25t Telefocus. 25b John Price. 26 Robin Kerrod. 28 Sci Pix. 29 The Marconi Company Ltd. 30 John Walmsley. 31t PP. 31b SPL/Jerome Yeats. 33 Paul Brierley. 34 Zefa/Tom Tracy. 35l RF/Images by Goodman. 35r Sci Pix. 35b RF. 36 PP. 38t SCL. 38bl Ann Ronan Picture Library. 38br Peter Newark's Western Americana. 39 SPL/Dr Jeremy Burgess. 40 PP. 41 Canon. 42l Sony. 42r Margaret Coreau.